Abusing the Public Trust:

An Inside Look at Reintegration Under the KSVPA

Manufactured in the United States of America. Copyright 2024) by Dustin Merryfield. All rights reserved. No part of this book may be reproduced in any form, audio, digital, or in print, except excerpts by reviewers, without written permission from the copyright holder or Cadmus Publishing LLC.

DISCLAIMER:
The thoughts, opinions, and expressions herein are those of the author and do not reflect those of Cadmus Publishing LLC. Any similarities to actual events or people are purely coincidental. Names and distinguishing characteristics may have been changed to preserve identities of any individuals.
Published by Cadmus Publishing LLC. P. O. Box 8664. Haledon, NJ 07538

Web: Cadmuspublishing.com
Web: BooksByPrisoners.com
Business email: admin@cadmuspublishing.com
Author email: info@cadmuspublishing.com
Phone: 360.565.6459
ISBN# 978-1-63751-455-9
Book catalog info. Categories.

CadmusPublishing.com

Previous Works

Sexually Violent Predator an Inside Look Into the KSVPA Statute and Facility, Published 2022

Thanks

Ultimate praise is to God for giving me the talents and abilities in the world that I have today. In addition to God many people here on earth have assisted me greatly in my endeavors.

My mother, a big supporter, brought me into this world and raised me the best she could. As to the stepfathers in my life I am grateful for what they have done.

To all the professionals, who have provided me either therapy or education, which gave me the tools to be able to do what I have done and present this material.

Lastly thank you to Cadmus Publishing for providing the services to publish and make my book available, when others would not.

I am gracious and look forward to putting out more books in the near future.

Table of Contents

Introduction 1

Abbreviations 3

The Definition of Reintegration

Chapter 1: The Legal Definition 6

Chapter 2: The KDADS Definition 8

How to Attain Reintegration Status

Chapter 1: Introduction 12

Chapter 2: Release by KDADS 13

Chapter 3:   Statutory Release 21

Preparing for Reintegration

Chapter 1:   Introduction 24

Chapter 2:   Cell Phone 25

Chapter 3:   Internet 28

Chapter 4:   Automobile 34

Chapter 5:   Logbooks 37

Chapter 6:   Medication 39

Chapter 7:   Meals 42

Chapter 8:   Support Network 44

Chapter 9:   Financial 47

Chapter 10:   College/Job Skills 54

Chapter 11:   Laundry 57

Chapter 12:   What is Taught 59

The Rules in Reintegration

Chapter 1:	Introduction	63
Chapter 2:	The 2017 Version	65
Chapter 3:	The 2018 Version	110

Disciplinary Process

Chapter 1: Introduction 144

Chapter 2: Notifications Received 146

Chapter 3: Due Process 220

Paying for Reintegration

Chapter 1:	Introduction	224
Chapter 2:	Rent at Reintegration	226
Chapter 3:	Secure Confinement	228

The Human Workforce

Chapter 1:	Introduction	232
Chapter 2:	Secure Confinement	233
Chapter 3:	Rules	240

Return from Reintegration

Chapter 1:	Introduction	245
Chapter 2:	Boundary Issue	249
Chapter 3:	The Risk Posed	258
Chapter 4:	Why Not Report	260
Chapter 5:	The Sentence	266
Chapter 6:	Her Consequence	268

Back to Secure Confinement

Chapter 1:	Introduction	270

| Chapter 2: | Therapy vs. Discipline | 271 |
| Chapter 3: | Media | 277 |

Past, Present, and Future Verbal Boundary Violations

Chapter 1:	Introduction	280
Chapter 2:	Prior to Reintegration	281
Chapter 3:	During Reintegration	283
Chapter 4: Time	At Secure Confinement, the Second	285

Past, Present, and Future Visual Boundary Violations

Chapter 1:	Introduction	291
Chapter 2:	Prior to Reintegration	293
Chapter 3:	During Reintegration	295
Chapter 4: Time	At Secure Confinement, the Second	296

Double Standard Concerning Boundary Violation

| Chapter 1: | The Incident | 299 |

Potential Victim

Chapter 1:	Introduction	302
Chapter 2:	Television	303
Chapter 3:	Internet	304
Chapter 4:	In the Community	306
Chapter 5:	The Purpose of Treatment	308

E-Mail in Reintegration

| Chapter 1: | The Consequence of E-Mail | 312 |

Kansas Offender Registration Act

Chapter 1:	Introduction	315
Chapter 2:	The KORA	316
Chapter 3:	Legal Battles Over KORA	405
Chapter 4:	The Cost of KORA	409
Final Thoughts		411

Introduction

For me I am able to admit that I lived a past wherein I offended others. This led to my incarceration as a juvenile and then eventually adult prison.

When I left adult prison I was tried under the Kansas Sexually Violent Predator Act, K.S.A. 59-29a01 et seq. Once committed, I spent about eighteen years in the program before I was removed from secure confinement to reintegration. Technically the Courts call Reintegration, secure confinement, but this is a myth that this book is meant to dispel.

For the citizens of Kansas and other States this means that the entrusted officers ignore the laws as the legislature has put in place. Though this does not mean you are safe, it does mean that there may be an expense, for it could be abuse of a person that has been entrusted to their care.

Secrets in my life are what allowed offending. I believe that transparency is key and I know society does not care about a predator. However, I believe that they will care about the process called Reintegration. It is for this reason I bring this book.

Pre-Release: Reintegration

Enjoy reading about Reintegration and when done if you are so inclined or motivated to make a difference feel free to contact the right person.

Abbreviations

In this book there will be abbreviations used for certain terms. In order to understand these we include a quick reference here for them.

- A. KDADS – Kansas Department on Aging and Disability Services. The State Agency with statutory control over the entire KSVPA.
- B. KSVPA – Kansas Sexually Violent Predator Act, K.S.A. § 59-29a01 et seq.
- C. PRP – Progress Review Panel. Statutorily defined in K.S.A. 59-29a02(j).
- D. PV – Used solely in Reintegration. Means Potential Victim. Reintegration uses this term to refer to every child in the world whether or not they are in the person's attraction template. It does not mean a potential victim for the person, unless it meets their pattern of offending.
- E. SRS – Social and Rehabilitation Services, the entity that was in control of the treatment program under the KSVPA, prior to KDADS.
- F. RPP – Relapse Prevention Plan.

G. IT – Information Technology, a department utilized by KDADS or SRS to maintain and keep their computer systems operational.

H. KDOC – Kansas Department of Corrections, the entity responsible for housing those under sentence of criminal conviction.

I. KOP – Keep On Person, refers to a term by KDOC whereby an individual keeps and is responsible for their own medication.

J. VTP – Vocational Training Program.

The Definition of Reintegration

Pre-Release: Reintegration

Chapter 1: The Legal Definition

The KSVPA was created in 1994, since its inception, it only speaks of three levels of confinement: (1) Secure Confinement; (2) Transitional Release; and (3) Conditional Release. These are stated and defined in the statutes that comprise the KSVPA. Now you are asking yourself what then is Reintegration?

Around the year 2007 the entity in charge under the KSVPA, the Kansas SRS, opened a part of their Osawatomie State Hospital to be what it deemed a Reintegration Facility under the KSVPA.

Today there are three reintegration facilities: (1) Osawatomie, Kansas; (2) Parsons, Kansas; and (3) Larned, Kansas. I spent my Reintegration time at Parsons, Kansas.

The first challenge to Reintegration came in 2011. The Court of Appeals, *In re Twilleger,* 46 Kan. App. 2d 302, held that Reintegration was an internal move within Secure Confinement and was not Transition.

The KSVPA, specifically, K.S.A. 59-29a02(i), since the decision in *Twilleger*, defines Transition as: "Transitional release means any halfway house, work release, sexually violent predator treatment facility or other placement designed to assist the person's adjustment and reintegration into the community."

The State of Kansas has never defined or put a legal definition of Reintegration in the KSVPA. The term is solely an internal term of KDADS, and was interpreted by the Kansas Court of Appeals.

Chapter 2: The KDADS Definition

Now that we know the law does not define Reintegration, what does the agency in charge define it as?

The first definition KDADS uses is found in its internal Policy titled 6.1 Treatment. It holds: "Tier Three takes place at one of the reintegration facilities currently housed on the grounds of Larned State Hospital (Meyer House East), Osawatomie State Hospital (MiCo), and Parsons State Hospital (Maple House and Willow House). These facilities are designed to offer residents on Tier Three of SPTP and Transitional Release a safe, step-by-step way of moving into an outpatient mode of functioning. These facilities allow residents to demonstrate their ability to manage the responsibilities of an independent, responsible lifestyle and to make good judgments in a variety of real world situations, while still operating under the support of SPTP supervision."

Once a person is moved to a Reintegration facility they are issued a rulebook. While in Reintegration I received two rule books. They define Reintegration as follows:

Reintegration Facility Rulebook January 2017

> "The SPTP Reintegration Facilities are State funded programs located at Larned State Hospital, Osawatomie State Hospital and Parsons State Hospital and Training Center. A Reintegration Facility (RF) accepts Residents who have been determined by the Progress Review Panel (PRP) to meet all of the requirements necessary for transition from Larned State Hospital's Sexual Predator Treatment Program."

Reintegration Facility Rulebook August 2018

> "The Sexual Predator Treatment Program (SPTP) Reintegration Facilities are located at Larned State Hospital (LSH), Osawatomie State Hospital (OSH) and Parsons State Hospital and Training Center (PSHTC). A Reintegration Facility (RF) accepts Residents who the Progress Review Panel (PRP) determined to have satisfied all requirements necessary for transition from the secured SPTP facility at LSH to a less therapeutic setting of a RF."

The two rule books issued in Reintegration define and state that Reintegration is what the statues in Kansas call "transition."

In 2018 the Secretary from KDADS submitted an annual review report to the committing court and stated I was in transition, not reintegration. A clear statement that even the Secretary of KDADS recognizes reintegration as being transition.

From the State's documentation and actions it is clear that reintegration is transition. As to the Courts in Kansas it remains secure confinement.

Pre-Release: Reintegration

How to Attain Reintegration Status

Chapter 1: Introduction

The term Reintegration is defined to mean the period of release from the secure confinement portion of the KSVPA. How does one earn this status?

In order to properly discuss this we have to look at two situations: (1) Release by KDADS; and (2) The statutorily proper method of release to transition.

Each of the methods for placing one on reintegration status is different and unique. They are not similar or equal in any fashion.

Chapter 2: Release by KDADS

When a person is committed by the Court under the KSVPA they are transported and delivered to the treatment facility. Upon arrival at the facility the individual will have access to the rules and policies of the facility.

The policy concerning treatment is titled Policy 6.1 Treatment. In accords with this policy the treatment program is separated into tiers, a total of three.

Prior to starting on a tier an assessment will be made. This is to determine if the individual will be Mainstream or Parallel Program. Individuals with intellectual disabilities or other disabilities that hinder their learning process are assigned to the Parallel Program. Any person without this is assigned to the Mainstream Program.

The assessment also determines, based on the Risk Needs Responsivity (RNR) model, which one of three risk levels, high, medium, and low, the person will be on. By policy high risk is to receive three hours of group therapy a week, medium risk is to receive two hours of group therapy per week, and low risk is to receive one hour of group therapy per week.

The risk level nor the assignment to parallel or mainstream changes how the tiers operate or how to advance. Let's look at the tier system for more clarification.

Tier one is known as skill acquisition. The purpose of this Tier is to provide necessary skills to the person through groups and other therapy classes. The person will also be required to pass two polygraphs (Victim and Behavior) before being allowed to request advancement to Tier 2. Tier 1 takes no less than one year to complete.

If the person believes he is ready for advancement to Tier 2 he can submit a request to treatment Team and Clinical Team to see the Progress Review Panel (PRP). The PRP is the only entity with the authority to progress one in treatment, in accords with KDADS' rules or policies.

Treatment Team meets once per week and is comprised of any staff of the facility that wants to attend. The participants are different each week and can include therapists, licensed medical personnel, program directors, social workers, floor staff, etc.

Clinical only meets once a month, and sometimes more. In order to attend clinical one must be a licensed clinician. This can include social workers, therapists, psychologists, etc.

In addition to receiving approval from Treatment Team and Clinical the individual has eight criteria that he must meet in order to meet with the PRP. KDADS sets these criteria in Policy 6.2 Progress Review Panel.

The facility sets the first requirement as: "Resident must not have received any notifications for physical or verbal aggression, sexual misconduct or serious rule violations (this would be anything of a serious nature)." This seems straightforward and objective, however, it is not.

In the facility they have adopted a system whereby they provide a classification for a rule violation, yes it is similar to that found in the Department of Corrections. This means a Class I rule violation is the most serious and often is a felony violation of the law. A Class II rule violation is moderately serious and includes what would be a misdemeanor under the law. A Class III rule violation is considered the lowest with barely any serious nature to it at all.

If the person receives a Class III rule violation they are denied the ability to see the PRP or advance. Further, if the Resident admits during a polygraph to a Class III rule violation and receives no notification he is still denied the ability to see the PRP. How can all classes of rule violations be of such a serious nature that advancement is denied? Are they seeking only perfect humans? This is very subject and apparently guaranteed to ensure one fails.

The second and third requirement concern polygraphs within the facility. Yes, a polygraph is mandatory every six months in order to progress through the treatment program. The criteria for both of these are: (2) "Resident must have completed a Victim polygraph and Sexual History polygraph with results of "No Significant Reaction" (3) Resident must have had at least two consecutive polygraphs, to include the Victim, Sexual History and/or Monitor polygraphs, during the past year with results of "No Significant Reactions."

These two requirements are very objective. If one passes the polygraphs, they are allowed to seek advancement if they meet the other criteria.

The fourth requirement is that the person will not have engaged in inappropriate sexual behaviors during the past six months. This is very subjective as it requires self-reporting. What if the person is playing the game and keeping these hidden? What harm could or would this cause? One may be desperate to advance, thereby causing him not to report. If advanced based on an improper self-report what harm will occur. Is it isolated to the person or will the public be affected?

The fifth requirement is that the person will not have had any inappropriate sexual fantasies without using immediate interventions during the previous year. This is very subjective as it requires self-reporting. What if the person is playing the game and keeping these hidden? What harm could or would this cause? One may be desperate to advance, thereby causing him not to report. If advanced based on an improper self-report what harm will occur. Is it isolated to the person or will the public be affected?

The sixth requirement is that the person regularly turns in sexual fantasy logs and journals to their therapist for the previous six months. This is an objective goal. However, this is no longer followed in that the therapists decided to no longer receive journals, instead they require that RSA's be turned in.

The seventh requirement is that the person completes and turns in a Relapse Prevention Plan (RPP). One could look at this as objective, but the facility and practices of the therapists in the facility make it subjective.

Let's look at a classic example, one I have seen multiple times, using a fictional character. Joe turns in a RPP and is advanced to tier two because his therapist approved of the RPP. About six months later Joe is reduced to tier one for fighting. Upon this digression he is assigned to a therapist he has not had before. After nine months Joe requests to advance back to tier two and is denied for the therapist has an issue with his RPP. Why was it good enough to advance previously, but it is not now? That is because a human, therapist, is involved making the criteria subjective. There is no method to ensure that what once was good enough will remain so.

To go even further there is no universal standard as to what a RPP is or what it must contain. Each therapist is free to come up with their own thoughts, ideas or requirements.

By allowing this through the human element it makes the criteria subjective.

The final requirement is that the person's therapist must recommend advancement. This means a person's views, thoughts, and beliefs color the process and control over any sort of an objective reason or purpose. This is subjective for the human element is involved. What if the therapist dislikes the person? What if there is retaliation for a past event? Why should the person have to remain confined because of a dislike by a therapist?

If one meets meet all the criteria Treatment Team and Clinical more than likely will allow him to see the PRP and have a chance to advance. In the end one must do this at least twice: once for tier two and then for tier three, Reintegration.

Once the person completes Tier 1 and is allowed to advance he is placed on Tier 2. Tier 2 is aptly named Skill Demonstration. The goal of this tier is for the confined person to transition from a structured inpatient program to an independent lifestyle. This occurs by participating in the Good Lives Model, self-regulation group and therapy group. There are no set time requirements for the groups on this tier.

Pre-Release: Reintegration

On tier two the confined person begins Reintegration by going out on supervised community outings. There are a minimum of thirteen community outings that must be completed. These are: (1) Minimum of three on-campus outings; (2) Minimum of three off-campus dining outings; (3) Minimum of seven off-campus shopping/activity outings; and (4) Maintenance outings as needed.

Based on outings Tier 2 is no less than fourteen months in length. Once the person completes the supervised community outings they may apply for Tier 3 if they meet the eight criteria previously discussed. In addition they must be financially set and have a certain amount of money on hand. If approved they are then advanced to Tier 3 and moved to a Reintegration facility.

This completes how one can garner release to reintegration from KDADS.

Chapter 3: Statutory Release

The KSVPA states that after secure confinement is transitional release. It states three methods for one to achieve transition status: (1) At an annual review hearing; (2) If the Secretary of KDADS files a request stating the person should be in transition; and (3) The person, if they have evidence, may petition the Court at any time.

No matter which one of the three methods is used the committing court first has to hold a trial and if it is determined that the person is safe they may be released to transition.

The KSVPA defines Transition as: ""Transitional release means any halfway house, work release, sexually violent predator treatment facility or other placement designed to assist the person's adjustment and reintegration into the community."

By definition Transition is when one leaves Secure Confinement and begins taking part in the everyday activities of a person in society. These activities can be stated to be: grocery shopping, having a job, going fishing, going to the casino, etc. As the person is in society with no control upon him the KSVPA requires the Court to determine that the person has changed that the public would not be in danger by him being on Transition. KDADS' use of Reintegration usurps this requirement and allows KDADS to put one in the community without the Court first finding if the person has changed.

If one has attained Transition after a Court proceeding then they are not able to be returned to Secure Confinement without the Court first holding a hearing and determining that the person has digressed and now presents a danger. This method of checks and balances is skirted by KDADS' use of Reintegration, where they return one to Secure Confinement any time they feel like it without oversight by the Court or impartial person or entity.

In review do we want an entity taking the power from the Court? Or should it remain with the Court? The State via KDADS wants to leave the Court out, but as a tax payer our representatives in the Kansas Legislature want it to remain with the Court. As such it should be left with the Court.

Preparing For Reintegration

Chapter 1: Introduction

Reintegration requires the individual to be ready for many of life's ordinary tasks, that which one who has been confined may not know well or at all. This includes laundry, meal preparation, financial, driving, and more.

As these are ordinary incidents of life one would believe that the treatment in the Secure Confinement would prepare and assist one in learning these basic skills, however, it cannot be said to be true.

To complicate matters even more the individuals confined have spent more than half, or at times all of their adult life in confinement. Therefore, they lack these basic skills that are needed in today's society.

For a clearer picture we will discuss each in detail and show where it would not be an issue to enact a change for one to be more prepared for society. This then leads to success upon release and a reduction of danger.

Chapter 2: Cell Phone

Over the last few years telecommunication has went from a land line to a portable line known as a cellular telephone.

Over time individuals in society learn the ins and outs of the new telecommunication device and what it can do. For example, the smart phone, non-smart phone, internet, no internet, data usage, and texting.

Think of one who has been in confinement for the last twenty plus years and the only experience they have is with a land line. For those who may not know what a land line is, it was the phone that every household had that was not portable, had no video and could not text. How are they to know what cell phone to buy, what the best option is, or what they should have?

On his first day in Reintegration he is required to get a cell phone. There are no classes or instruction provided as to what he should look for, what to expect and/or what the cost would be. The Secure Confinement makes cell phones contraband, a felony offense in Kansas.

Pre-Release: Reintegration

As it is a felony in Kansas one is unable to gain literature and try to learn the cellular telecommunication device on his own. One who wants to better prepare is denied the ability.

Then in Reintegration one is provided no training or education he is just expected to purchase one outright the first day or two he is there. You may say well that is how one in society learned?

For some that is true, but for most they grew up around it and someone who could guide and help them know what to look for, then they would have used one and known how to operate it. So, why are the ones under the KSVPA kept from modern technology?

The basic answer is to cripple their chance at success when released. In fact this has been proven for a high number of those returned to Secure Confinement from Reintegration are due to violating the rules concerning a cell phone.

I argue a change needs to be made. Secure Confinement can not only teach the basics of cell phones, but at the second stage of treatment they should allow for one to have a cell phone and show the skills they learned in the first

Pre-Release: Reintegration

stage of treatment. This is how KDADS structured their program to work or operate, why not allow for it?

Chapter 3: Internet

In today's society the computer, more specifically, the internet is a daily use item that is necessary. In Secure Confinement they do not provide any computer skills and when asked why the answer received was IT does not allow us to do that.

Most individuals in Secure Confinement was not out when computers were modern tools and most definitely when the internet became as necessary as it is today. Therefore, they cannot operate a computer or even the internet. Why is this valuable skill not provided or taught in Secure Confinement?

Even if it were taught in Secure Confinement there are necessary parts of the internet that one in Reintegration cannot use. One in Reintegration is not allowed any social media site use or accounts. In addition the individual cannot use analog internet to avoid pictures, pop ups or ads, but will be disciplined when they appear.

Analog Internet

You may be asking yourself, what is analog internet? When I was learning computers back in the 90's they taught what they called analog internet. This is internet without any images making it text based internet only.

In most web browsers one can turn the images off (Analog Internet On) with a simple click of a button. In the Reintegration Facility I received several write ups for having images show up on the internet. Your first question is, if I knew about this why did I not turn the images off? The simple answer is that is not allowed without the Director's permission.

I did request permission on several occasions and was denied. I even went so far as to print out the instructions for the web browser to show that it was a simple click of the button and was denied the ability to turn off the pictures. The question now may be, why? To me it was only so they could stack up and increase the number of write ups given, but this is a judgment of mine. Let's look at some facts of the situation.

In Reintegration the web browser was Google Chrome®, which does allow for analog Internet. I requested to use analog Internet and was denied, but never given a reason as to why the denial was given. In fact I even printed off the simple instructions for how to turn it on and was still denied. In Google Chrome® you turn it on by: (1) Click the customize/control Google Chrome Button> Settings; (2) Click show advanced settings; (3) In the privacy section click content settings; and (4) In the image section select do not show images. Once these steps are completed just click OK to validate.

Pioneering SVP Programs

In Washington State the legislature has made inroads in pioneering methods to ensure that those confined under their SVP act have computer and internet skills. They also did it to halt or prevent prohibited, banned, or illegal material. This was declared by their legislature to be essential to achieve therapeutic goals.

"The legislature finds there have been ongoing, egregious examples of certain residents of the special commitment center having illegal child pornography, other prohibited pornography, and other banned materials on their computers. The legislature also finds that activities at the special commitment center must be designed and implemented to meet treatment goals of the special commitment center, and proper and appropriate computer is one such activity. The legislature also finds that by linking computer usage to treatment plans, residents are less likely to have prohibited materials on their computers and are more likely to successfully complete their treatment plans. Therefore, the legislature finds that resident's computer usage in compliance with conditions placed on computer usage is essential to achieving their therapeutic goals. If residents' usage of computers is not in compliance or is not related to meeting their treatment goals, computer usage will be limited in order to prevent or reduce residents' access to prohibited materials." [2010 c 218 § 1.]

In Washington they have seen a reduction in contraband while allowing their residents to be rehabilitated and familiar with the main part of society, computers and internet. Should not the same be true in Kansas?

Conclusion

Now let's take a deeper look at this issue. In Secure Confinement all Internet access, and for the most part computer access, is completely denied. Most of the individuals confined under the KSVPA have no computer knowledge and went to lock up prior to the existence of the Internet. As this is a common skill today it should be a skill (tool) that is taught and provided to see how they deal with it. But it is not. In my mind, this is the first failure of Secure Confinement.

In fact in or around the year 2009 Internet and E-Mail was provided to persons confined in the Kansas Department of Corrections, even sex offenders. The KDOC ensures that those it confines knows the tools of modern society and is able to use them for those that are being punished. Civil commitment under the KSVPA is not punitive, so why are they provided less?

The purpose of Reintegration is to acclimate the person to society. As such since the Secure Confinement does not provide Internet training or skills, should Reintegration not be required to just start with analog Internet? As parents in the world do today, a child is not just given unfettered access to the Internet their first time. The same should be true in Reintegration.

Failing to do this shows the intent is to let the person be written up and disciplined and not be allowed to use anything to mitigate, comply with, or be in accords with the rules. This is based on the fact that one cannot control what shows on the Internet.

Upon return to Secure Confinement I presented the denial of analog Internet to different therapists and they cannot understand why I was not allowed to use a tool that would allow me to remain compliant with the rules and exert some control. This would have shown that I had changed and was not trying to be the same as I was in the past. I argue that just requesting analog Internet shows that I changed and wanted to do right.

One should question why one cannot use the tools he knows or has learned while in Reintegration? Unless the intent is for the person to fail this should not be denied.

Chapter 4: Automobile

In today's world the automobile is a necessity. The automobile allows one to work, travel, get medical care, and is involved in almost every aspect of one's life. The question is whether or not one is prepared for this prior to being placed in Reintegration.

For most, a person grows up learning the skill of an automobile and the particulars (i.e. insurance, gas, taxes, licensing, etc.). for some confined under the KSVPA this is untrue and most lack such knowledge, and for those that returned this growing it has been many years and they are out of touch with this.

Under the KSVPA the entity in control has defined the first part of treatment to be skill acquisition. First thought is that one lacking will acquire the skills to be effective with an automobile, however, this is not true. In its entirety the treatment program provides no knowledge or skill teaching concerning automobiles.

The truth is that the individual is faced with purchasing and operating a motor vehicle once they get to

Reintegration. Yes, the treatment program refused to provide any preparation for this in the first two parts of treatment.

While in Reintegration the individual is provided no training or guidance in the purchase or operation of an automobile. When the individual reaches the ability to have an automobile they are to figure out on their own how to get a license, purchase the automobile and start driving. Reintegration could be correct if the first part, Skill Acquisition, did its part, but it does not.

Now the individual is in a high stress situation which is critical. Studies show that when in a high stress situation these individuals are more likely to offend. Now the State has reverted the individual back to a risk of re-offense, hope the rest of treatment was better. Now the State has created a risk.

Now we assume that the individual overcomes all of these hurdles, does not re-offend, and now is an owner and driver of an automobile. Can there be more consequences to the individual or society as a whole? The answer is yes.

In order to get the automobile the individual more than likely had to finance it, put it on a payment plan. If the entity in control returns the person back to secure confinement, they will have to forfeit the automobile, their payment plan, and cause the financing entity a loss.

The finance company, due to a loss, then passes it on to their consumers (Rate hikes, etc.) and their shareholders, if any. This effects society as a whole and for the individual wrecks their credit.

As to the automobile there is no Skill Acquisition provided and no training prior to going to Reintegration, or while at Reintegration. This is a danger and as a society we should expect more of those we entrust to provide care and treatment.

Chapter 5: Logbooks

When the word logbook comes up what is your first idea? Well that is probably not what a logbook is in Reintegration. In Reintegration they require that one record in a logbook every phone call made, every trip they make, and everything they do.

At first glimpse this does not seem like a bad thing or one that is too complicated. However, it has caused a many to want to return due to the stress it brings.

The logbook requires perfection and not one mistake is forgiven or over looked. An example of this is provided in the section of this book titled "Disciplinary Process" "Chapter 2: Notifications Received." They compare each logbook to the phone statement once per month and all must be logged. For a normal citizen they answer the phone or receive a text and give no thought, but one in Reintegration must also log it or be punished.

In preparing the logbook they require: (1) Chronological order; (2) Different color ink for each type (phone call, travel, text, etc.) of entry; (3) Receipts must be attached; and (4) The entries be clear and legible. Remember no excuses and no mistakes.

Though it can be said to be a vital tool that helps one track time and other important things, the logbook is new for the person. They do not teach it in the skill acquisition phase of treatment and then do not require it on the application phase of treatment. The person is required to begin it at Reintegration without fail and without training only to be consequented for any error or mistakes in it no matter how small.

As to the logbook there is no skill acquisition provided and no training prior to going to Reintegration, or while at Reintegration. This is a danger and as a society we should expect more of those we entrust to provide care and treatment.

Chapter 6:   Medication

As you read this chapter keep in mind that Reintegration is meant to prepare one to return to society and how to function as a citizen. As such as you read, ask yourself if what is required, is a part of your of your daily routine.

Medication is defined in Reintegration as an over the counter, prescribed, or other item meant to heal an ailment or condition. It does include salves, ointments, and other beauty products they deem to have a medicinal effect.

In secure confinement they declare that medication, the same definition as Reintegration, is contraband. This is so the point that individuals have and do receive severe consequences for having a band-aid in their room.

As a kid growing up in institutions I was to be responsible for the purchase and use of any and all medications, except that which is on the controlled narcotics list. Then, when I went to KDOC, the same was true and they called it KOP. In fact all of the men confined under the KSVPA went to KDOC and the same was true for them. This taught responsibility.

Pre-Release: Reintegration

Upon entering secure confinement under the KSVPA it was made clear that all medication was contraband. In order to get it I have to see a doctor; get a prescription; and wait for a licensed person to dispense it to me. This is true even for Tylenol. The cost for each licensed person is a tax to the citizens of society, is it necessary?

Remember the first part of treatment is skill acquisition therefore if someone cannot properly manage their medication should this not be taught? In addition how did all of these men do it in KDOC? It appears that the facility is bleeding funds from the tax payers unnecessarily.

The second part of treatment is application of the skills acquired, however the rules concerning medication do not change. How then can the program know if it will be a issue before putting the person in society?

The third part of treatment, Reintegration, is the first time the person will again be responsible for their medication and it not be considered contraband. This though brings with it many issues.

In Reintegration they require that medication no matter what it is be tracked and listed on a specific log sheet.

This log sheet has to be adjusted every time one pill or item be used. Once per month an inspection will be had, and any errors on the sheet will bring severe consequences that can include a return to the first part of treatment.

This causes stress for the individual for: (1) It is a new procedure; (2) Perfection is required; and/or (3) It can only be avoided by using no medication. This leads to health problems and can lead to re-offense.

The author is unaware of any citizen in society that is required to perfectly log their medications and allow such records to be subjected to review that can cause them to be confined if wrong. In addition, why are the taxpayers paying for such a situation? Money is tight and to do like KDOC and the juvenile facilities would save millions of dollars.

Chapter 7: Meals

One very basic life requirement is eating. In order for this to occur one needs to know how to cook or how to plan to pay for another (fast food, restaurant, etc.) to do this for them.

Under KSVPA the average stay is no less than five years. When one adds that to the time in prison it averages about ten years. One would think the skill acquisition phase of treatment would assess whether one has the knowledge/skills to select and prepare their own meals, but this is a myth.

In the facility under KSVPA the following is true: (1) No assessment is made; (2) No class is provided to teach cooking; and (3) There are many that lack the skills in this area. For me, I grew up learning to cook and am well versed in this skill.

When I went to Reintegration there was a fellow that was living on heat and eat items from a microwave, when I inquired why he told me he did not know how to cook. I set about teaching him and when I left he was pretty good.

In the area of meal preparation and budgeting the person under KSVPA fails to prepare one before sending them to Reintegration.

Chapter 8: Support Network

A support network is a group of people that assist the person in leading an offense free life. The group can be made up of family, friends, associates, or professionals from all walks of life. The support network is a necessary and integral part of the RPP and the program teaches this the most.

As a necessary and integral part of treatment one would think that one confined under the KSVPA is provided ample opportunity to create and build a support network. The truth is that the facility structures itself to ensure that one cannot create or build a support network.

When I spent time in KDOC I had the ability to use several different pen pal services to meet new people. This allowed the building blocks for a support network. Today inmates in KDOC continue this, but in a more sophisticated manner, E-Mail. Those under the KSVPA are denied E-Mail.

As the facility puts blanket bans in place to prevent meeting people via pen pal service a lawsuit was enacted. In the end the Kansas Court of Appeals held that those under the KSVPA have a constitutional right to pen pals. Their words were: "Most Americans do not give much thought to having a pen pal. For a civilly committed patient, a pen pal represents the ability to meet new people and potentially form new friend friendships; losing this ability is a significant and atypical hardship." *Merryfield v. Sullivan*, 2015 Kan. App. Unpub. Lexis 37, *9-10; 342 P. 3d 1; 2015 WL 326652.

Since the decision individuals have sought to use pen pal services and the program sticks to its blanket ban and enforces it with strict punishment. This is even true when the pen pal service allows:

1. For the facility to first approve and confirm any photo of the person they post on their service.
2. One to have to list their criminal history, confirmed by the facility.
3. For the ad they place, to be sent to the facility and monitored by the facility.

The most basic and fundamental way a confined person to meet new people is a pen pal. This is denied by the entity in control under KSVPA and in turn prevents the building or creation of a support network. Is this not then a denial of treatment?

If one cannot have pen pals, how are they to meet new people and inform them of who they are and enlist them to be part of their support network? There must be a mystical and magical way the therapists know that they are not making known to others.

It cannot be said that the skill acquisition phase of treatment that one has the ability to create and formulate a support network. This then means it cannot be tested or used in the application and demonstration phase of treatment. Thus, one goes to Reintegration unprepared and, more likely than not without a support network.

Chapter 9:   Financial

Everyone knows that money makes the world go round, it is necessary for everyday living. In Reintegration the individual has to buy everything (food, hygiene, clothing, medical, etc.) and then a car and house. Are they prepared for this?

In short terms the answer is no, but let's go further into this to know more. For this we will discuss: (1) The US PATRIOT Act; (2) KDOC; (3) Jobs; (4) Education and Training; and (5) Room and Board.

A.   The US PATRIOT Act.

In order to fight terrorism the United States Congress enacted the US PATRIOT Act. This Act requires one to have a government issued ID in order to open a financial account, including the most basic, checking and savings.

The entity in control of the KSVPA denies the one confined from getting a government ID thereby preventing them from having accounts or using services to build financials. Recently, year 2023, they started allowing a few to get a government ID if the person can afford it and has proper documents. These expire every year under the KORA, so we will see if the individuals continue to be able to have government ID.

The State of Washington has enacted within their SVP Act a mandate that the individual confined be granted government ID from the day they enter and it be renewed when required till the person leaves. Washington State Law 71.09.370. In doing this the law states that the person need not go to the licensing board (DMV in Kansas), rather an identification verification letter is sent then and ID is issued.

Other states have pioneered how to allow their individuals to have government ID, which allows for building a proper financial base but Kansas ensures one cannot by not finding or allowing a way to receive government ID.

B. KDOC

An inmate serving a sentence of punishment who makes minimum wage or more is required to have ten percent of all checks put into a savings account they cannot access until released. This is true even for one who has a life sentence and will never get out. This allows the inmate a firm financial foundation upon release.

Those confined under the KSVPA have no such thing and most lack the skills to save on their own. The facility does line their pockets by forcing the individual to pay half of their gross income each month.

The KSVPA facility withholds more from the confined person, but unlike KDOC it is to benefit the facility rather than the confined person.

C. Jobs

Prior to 2005 the individuals confined under the KSVPA were paid at a rate of three to four dollars per hour for jobs in the facility. After 2005 the individuals were paid minimum wage but had to pay half to the facility. This reverted them back to three to four dollars per hours.

Is it proper to have the individuals pay the facility or is it just a racket whereby the facility gets more money from taxpayers? It is tax dollars that provides the funds to pay the individuals.

It is true that most of the individuals do pay taxes each year. This provides for the cost of their stay, so is it just double taxation on a select group?

To understand the issue more let's look at a real example. An individual makes three hundred dollars a month, the facility deducts one-hundred and twenty-seven which leaves one hundred and seventy-three. This number is where they keep half or eighty-six dollars and fifty cents. At this rate for every one hundred employed they receive eight-thousand six hundred and fifty dollars extra from the tax payers.

If this was put in a mandatory saving plan for the individual, and he the recoups a mere 2.0% APY the person would earn fourteen cants a month, or at the end of the year would have one thousand forty-nine dollars and eleven cents. This means he made eleven dollars and eleven cents in interest.

As the individual spends an average of no less than five years before being released, he would have enough to be successful in Reintegration, but the added benefit to the taxpayers of having to pay taxes, which in effect means it will pay his wages with no burden on the taxpayers. The five year chart is:

Year 1

Month	Principal	Addition	Interest	Balance
1	$0.00	$86.50	$0.14	$86.64
2	$86.64	$86.50	$0.28	$173.43
3	$173.43	$86.50	$0.43	$260.35
4	$260.35	$86.50	$0.57	$347.42
5	$347.42	$86.50	$0.71	$434.64
6	$434.64	$86.50	$0.86	$521.99
7	$521.99	$86.50	$1.00	$609.49
8	$609.49	$86.50	$1.14	$697.14
9	$697.14	$86.50	$1.29	$784.93
10	$784.93	$86.50	$1.43	$872.86
11	$872.86	$86.50	$1.58	$960.94
12	$960.94	$86.50	$1.72	$1,049.16

Year 2

Month	Principal	Addition	Interest	Balance
13	$1,049.16	$86.50	$1.87	$1,137.52
14	$1,137.52	$86.50	$2.01	$1,226.04
15	$1,226.04	$86.50	$2.16	$1,314.69
16	$1,314.69	$86.50	$2.30	$1,403.50
17	$1,403.50	$86.50	$2.45	$1,492.45
18	$1,492.45	$86.50	$2.60	$1,581.54
19	$1,581.54	$86.50	$2.74	$1,670.78
20	$1,670.78	$86.50	$2.89	$1,760.17
21	$1,760.17	$86.50	$3.04	$1,849.71
22	$1,849.71	$86.50	$3.18	$1,939.39
23	$1,939.39	$86.50	$3.33	$2,029.22
24	$2,029.22	$86.50	$3.48	$2,119.20

Year 3

Month	Principal	Addition	Interest	Balance
25	$2,119.20	$86.50	$3.63	$2,209.33
26	$2,209.33	$86.50	$3.77	$2,299.60
27	$2,299.60	$86.50	$3.92	$2,390.02
28	$2,390.02	$86.50	$4.07	$2,480.59
29	$2,480.59	$86.50	$4.22	$2,571.31
30	$2,571.31	$86.50	$4.37	$2,662.18
31	$2,662.18	$86.50	$4.52	$2,753.20
32	$2,753.20	$86.50	$4.67	$2,844.37
33	$2,844.37	$86.50	$4.82	$2,935.69
34	$2,935.69	$86.50	$4.97	$3,027.15
35	$3,027.15	$86.50	$5.12	$3,118.77
36	$3,118.77	$86.50	$5.27	$3,210.54

Year 4

Month	Principal	Addition	Interest	Balance
37	$3,210.54	$86.50	$5.42	$3,302.46
38	$3,302.46	$86.50	$5.57	$3,394.53
39	$3,394.53	$86.50	$5.72	$3,486.75
40	$3,486.75	$86.50	$5.87	$3,579.13
41	$3,579.13	$86.50	$6.03	$3,671.65
42	$3,671.65	$86.50	$6.18	$3,764.33
43	$3,764.33	$86.50	$6.33	$3,857.16
44	$3,857.16	$86.50	$6.48	$3,950.14
45	$3,950.14	$86.50	$6.64	$4,043.28
46	$4,043.28	$86.50	$6.79	$4,136.57
47	$4,136.57	$86.50	$6.94	$4,230.01
48	$4,230.01	$86.50	$7.10	$4,323.61

Year 5

Month	Principal	Addition	Interest	Balance
49	$4,323.61	$86.50	$7.25	$4,417.36
50	$4,417.36	$86.50	$7.40	$4,511.26
51	$4,511.26	$86.50	$7.56	$4,605.32
52	$4,605.32	$86.50	$7.71	$4,699.53
53	$4,699.53	$86.50	$7.87	$4,793.90
54	$4,793.90	$86.50	$8.02	$4,888.42
55	$4,888.42	$86.50	$8.18	$4,983.10
56	$4,983.10	$86.50	$8.33	$5,077.93
57	$5,077.93	$86.50	$8.49	$5,172.92
58	$5,172.92	$86.50	$8.65	$5,268.07
59	$5,268.07	$86.50	$8.80	$5,363.37
60	$5,363.37	$86.50	$8.96	$5,458.83

The chart clearly shows that an average stay of five years would mean the person leaves with over five-thousand dollars to prepare for his re-entry to society. This is a good base, but instead KDADS takes and keeps this money for themselves.

Conclusion

There is the chance to be financially prepared for Reintegration, however, KDADS does all it can to block or thwart this. It even goes so far as lining their pockets with money at the expense of taxpayers, the mental well being of the individuals, and creating a plausible danger to society.

Chapter 10: College/Job Skills

In order to be successful one in society must have a job. The skills one has determines the type of job and even reduces the likelihood of one offending again in the future. Is there any preparation for this prior to Reintegration?

In KDOC if one does not have a high school diploma or G.E.D they are required to get one, though they can refuse. In addition KDOC provides college, vo-tech, and job skills. This is expensive for KDOC but a necessary part of rehabilitation. In fact this has been validated by an empirical study.

The University of Emory Department of Economics studied the effects an education has on recidivism rates, or likelihood to reoffend. They found: "An inmate that has at least some high school education recidivates at a rate of 55%. When the inmate adds some vocational training to his education toolbox, the offender's recidivism rate falls to 20%, and the rate continues to fall with each additional level of education. Again—quoting from a secondary report—Zoukis acknowledges that the recidivism rate is dramatically reduced when prisoner are afforded the opportunity of participating in post-secondary education. An inmate who earns an associate's degree presents a recidivism rate of only 13.7%; earning a bachelor's degree reduces that rate to 5.6%; and an inmate who earns a master's degree presents a recidivism rate of 0%." *Article: The Mind Oppressed: Recidivism as A Learned Behavior,* 6 Wake Forest J.L. & Pol'y 357"

Those confined under the KSVPA are denied the ability to get a G.E.D. or high school diploma if they do not have one. Further, they are denied the ability to receive a post-secondary education even if they want to pay for it for: (1) They have no ability to have a computer; (2) They have no internet; and (3) The facility refuses to work with them concerning a test proctor.

It is clear that one whose purpose of confinement is for punishment has better educational opportunities, whereas the confinement whose sole purpose is to reduce recidivism denies the most basic education.

The next part is job skills and whether or not any are provided or allowed. I came into the facility in the year 2000, since then inmates from KDOC have: (1) Worked on campus in dietary, laundry, maintenance, and the onsite restaurant to name a few; (2) Been allowed to freely walk anywhere on the campus; (3) Been allowed to drive state vehicles; and (4) Learn many trades while working on campus.

Those confined under the KSVPA are denied all that KDOC has. To keep this in focus it is appropriate to keep those on the first part of treatment within the secure perimeter. However those on the second part that go to restaurants and stores in the community to prepare for Reintegration, because a panel of experts found they changed and are safe, are even denied the job skills and physical conditioning that comes with the on-campus jobs.

For those confined in the KSVPA the jobs available to them is janitorial, cleaning a section of the building they live in. This is usually for one hour a day and no training is provided even though the job is listed as VTP.

To have the skills to find meaningful employment are denied to one confined under KSVPA, but is provided to one in KDOC for punishment.

Chapter 11:   Laundry

In the world today clothing is not optional, rather it is required in most all areas. As clothing is required there is a process known as laundry that is used to keep it clean and presentable.

As a kid in confinement I had to wash my own clothes or go without. This taught responsibility and financial management. The same as one required from day one in Reintegration.

In the confinement facility under KSVPA they treat laundry as a privilege and never require one to do their own laundry, learn how to do laundry, or learn the cost of doing laundry. You may ask how does one get clean clothes?

The facility uses taxpayer dollars to operate a large laundry facility. In fact said facility burned to the ground around the year 2008 and they asked the taxpayers for millions to rebuild it. Today it operates with a high expense they ask the taxpayers to pay for. The cost comes from: (1) The employees they pay to work there; (2) The cost of transporting to and from; (3) The inmates they employ; (4) The cost of supplies (soap, chemicals, etc.); (5) Paying for lost or damaged clothing;(6) the cost of linen; and (7) The equipment or machines; to name a few.

Laundry is a basic life skill and if treated as a requirement of treatment, which it should be, the money saved (millions) could be put to better use by the state.

Chapter 12:   What is Taught

Throughout this part of the book we have touched on eleven skills that the treatment facility, under the KSVPA, fails to teach before the person goes to Reintegration, though there are many more. This may cause you to wonder what is the taxpayers paying for?

The basic requirement of the program on the skill acquisition phase is that the individual will be in therapy for three hours a week. The requirement is one group, one therapist led class, and one psycho education class.

At an average annual cost of $68,000 per person confined, why is there only three hours of treatment on the skill acquisition phase? In addition what are these classes?

The group sessions and therapist led classes are held by licensed clinicians, whereas psychoeducation is taught by an Activity Therapist, a non-clinician that has a bachelor's degree.

Therapist led classes include (1) Relapse Prevention; (2) Cognitive Distortions; (3) Boundaries; (4) Emotional Intelligence; (5) PTSD; and (6) Dialectical Behavior Therapy; to name a few. In psychoeducation they offer (1) Rock Music;

(2) Country Music; (3) Speech; 94) Friedman's Fables; (5) Team Choices (Fantasy Role Playing); (6) Nutrition; (7) Communication; and (8) Basic Finance, managing a checking account; to name a few.

When one moves to the second phase of treatment, demonstration and application, they have the same classes with some that are only available on that stage, which are mandatory. These new mandatory classes are: (1) Simulated Life 1 & 2; (2) Tier Two Outings; (3) Community Reintegration; and (4) Job Skills; to name a few. This appears to be valid, however, appearances are not always correct.

Simulated Life 1 & 2 is a class where a person role plays a life with life events (job, car, etc.). They are given scenarios and have to show how they would handle it and are required to manage the finances for the person. However, it is not realistic and the leader has set it to be unrealistic. Some examples are; (1) The goat farmer has a scenario where an alien takes the goats; (2) One has to pay $650 a month for health insurance from work; and (3) There is no actual correct tax deduction; to name a few.

In all, no matter what the facility does, there is no assessment or evaluation at any level of treatment to determine what one needs or don't need. This causes one to be in a mandatory class he does not need. Then if for any reason the individual is dropped below the second tier, after completing the mandatory classes, he will be required to repeat those classes.

It is true that one who has been here for years, has to retake the same classes over and over again. The repeats have been empirically studied and shown to impede, block, or hinder treatment. There is no basic skills taught, but there are plenty of junk skills, like how to deal with aliens, that are taught. One therefore, is denied the ability to be prepared for Reintegration, let alone society and how it functions.

The Rules in Reintegration

Pre-Release: Reintegration

Chapter 1: Introduction

As with any facility there are always rules. The Reintegration facility has its own separate set of rules issued by KDADS. It can be said that this is contrary to state law, which requires one set of rules that are applicable to all confined under the KSVPA, or are being tried for the KSVPA. These requirements can be found at K.S.A. § 59-29a01 through § 59-29a27.

As it has its own rules and procedures those utilized in secure confinement are inapplicable. The most interesting ones are concerning media and property. This can be said to be in direct violation of the holding in *In re Twilleger,* 46 Kan. App. 2d 302, where the State of Kansas argued Reintegration was nothing more than an internal move within the secure confinement portion under the KSVPA, and the Court agreed.

One of the disagreements between secure confinement and Reintegration is personal property the person owns. Well if it is an internal move then why does the property not transfer without issue? In secure confinement a licensed therapist determines if it is permissible to have media (Music, Movies, Pictures, Video games, etc.), whereas in Reintegration a person with no degree or background in therapy determines whether media is appropriate. Often the decision at Reintegration is in opposition to a licensed therapist's decision. Thus, when an individual moves from Secure Confinement to Reintegration they incur the chance to have to lose personal property they have acquired. In the same fashion if returned to secure confinement one incurs the inability to have the property he had in Reintegration.

For more review I will now take you through review of the two rule books that were in effect when I was in Reintegration.

Pre-Release: Reintegration

Chapter 2: The 2017 Version

I arrived at Reintegration on June 5, 2018. At this time the facility was operating under a rule book that was dated January 2017.

To provide a transparent view of how the facility operates and what one could expect while in reintegration I have included it in its entirety, copied word for word.

SPTP Reintegration Facilities

The SPTP Reintegration Facilities are State funded programs located at Larned State Hospital, Osawatomie State Hospital and Parsons State Hospital and Training Center. A Reintegration Facility (RF) accepts Residents who have been determined by the Progress Review Panel (PRP) to meet all of the requirements necessary for transition from Larned State Hospital's Sexual Predator Treatment Program.

To be deemed ready for the program, Residents must have significantly changed their mental status, as evidenced by completion of the Tier 1 and 2, be recommended by the clinicians with whom the Resident works, and have a motivation to live a life free of crime. Residents must also

Pre-Release: Reintegration

interview with the PRP and be approved by the PRP for advancement to a Reintegration Facility.

Residents will obtain a job, if required, learn to budget and save money, and eventually live on their own in the community. Residents transition through the program on a Step System that allows them more and more freedom to make their own decisions and be on their own. The Reintegration Facilities supervise their Residents and empower them to make their own decisions and to learn from their mistakes. Our goal is to safely reintegrate Residents into the community and assist them in learning the skills to lead a life free of sexual offending.

Reasons why a Resident might be reduced a step or returned to LSH campus would include an established pattern of:

1. Not following rules, directives or regulations
2. Behavior problems
3. Not progressing, or regressing in therapy
4. Not actively participating in the program
5. Putting themselves in risky situation
6. Re-offending or committing other crimes

7. Possessing child pornography or other absolute contraband
8. Misuse of computers or other electronic equipment
9. A single incident of behavior which is seen as egregious
10. Any behavior which places the safety of the public or others at risk

**This list is not all inclusive

Program Guidelines:

RF Residents are given many responsibilities and privileges while at RF. Residents are expected to follow the rules set forth by the RF. Additionally, RF Residents are expected to be respectful, to be honest, and to be dedicated to their success in the program.

The following are general guidelines set forth for RF Residents:

- RF Residents are expected to be honest with RF Staff, Therapists, Parole Officer, Lawyers, Doctors and any other agency that the Resident has contact with at all times.

Pre-Release: Reintegration

- RF Residents are expected to have a good attitude. RF Residents are expected to be respectful of other Residents and the RF staff at all times. Arguing, yelling, cursing, name-calling and physical aggression are not appropriate ways of communicating. Serious consequences will result if this type of behavior is seen or reported which may include but is not limited to being served a rule violation report, receiving a step level loss, or possibly a return to LSH SPTP.

- RF Residents are expected to attend all appointments. This includes appointments that the Resident's schedule for themselves, therapy appointments, parole, shopping, support groups and any other appointment that RF staff have scheduled for the Residents.

- Depending on their Treatment Plan, RF Residents are expected to obtain employment while at RF. If a Resident is unable to find employment or is unable to work, they will be required to participate in approved volunteer work or other approved activities.

- Residents are expected to attend work regularly. RF Residents are expected to be on time and at work as scheduled. Any days that are to be missed **must** be cleared through the RF Director and the Resident's employer.

- RF Residents will be expected to ask permission to check their mail. Mail can be sent out via RF office mail. RF Residents are required to open each piece of mail in front of a RF staff. Any items deemed inappropriate by RF staff will be confiscated for review by the Director. If contraband has been identified/collected in the mail review process, the items will be destroyed and/or turned over to Law Enforcement.

- RF Residents are expected to obtain a cell phone (without a camera or camera has been disabled) while at RF. Residents will be required to log each incoming and outgoing phone call on the cell phone as well as the landline in each Resident's living area. Residents are expected to note in their provided call log who the call was to or from. Residents will submit their phone bill to the Director of the RF for review. The phone bill must be submitted at the time it is received.

Reintegration Facility Rules:

Note: If rules are changed/amended, Residents will be notified as such via a memo.

Resident Initials	
	1. Follow all stipulations of transition as outlined by the State of Kansas.
	2. Follow all the conditions of transitional release, if applicable.
	3. Complaints or comments in regards to Reintegration Facility rules or directives must be addressed in a proper manner. Complaining of or challenging rules will not be tolerated.

	4. Residents will complete a financial disclosure and sliding scale form and update these forms annually or when the Resident's economic status changes. Residents must disclose any and all personal assets currently in their name that they acquired prior to admission to the SPTP program or set up after their admission to the SPTP program.
	5. Residents will address staff respectfully, using proper names and/or titles. Residents will refrain from using derogatory terms when referring to staff or staff actions.

6. The use of aggression both physical (hitting, kicking, biting, pinching, spitting, etc.) and verbal (cussing, yelling, demanding) is an inappropriate way to get needs met or to solve problems. In addition a Resident's use of aggression may affect other Resident's treatment and compromises the safety and security of Resident's and staff. Any use of aggression is unacceptable.

7. In each resident room, residents will have phones provided to them, which they will answer every time staff call regardless of time or place. Phones are for local service only. Residents will be subject to random checks by phone as well as in person, and need to answer the phone or appear in person when checked on.

8. Residents are required to purchase a cell phone and set up an account in their own name before proceeding past Step 1A. residents are responsible for paying for their

personal cell phone bills monthly. Residents are to keep their cell phones with them at all times while in the community, at the Reintegration facility and keep them on so that they may receive or make calls. When required to call and check-in with Reintegration Facility staff, Residents must talk with a staff member. Leaving a message is unacceptable.

9. All Resident belongings will be inventoried upon arrival at the Reintegration Facility. Residents are responsible for informing staff of items purchased or brought into the building that are worth more than $10. Those items will be added to the Resident's inventory list that is located in the staff office. The Reintegration facility is not liable for items that are not disclosed to Reintegration facility staff. Major purchases (furniture, vehicle, etc.) or purchases made with a credit card must be approved by

Pre-Release: Reintegration

	Reintegration Facility management before purchasing the item.
	10. Residents will remain in the building at all times unless staff gives approval otherwise. Residents must have staff permission to be on the porch, center courtyard, or patios. No Resident will be permitted near any office window at any time while outside.
	11. When a Resident wishes to travel off the grounds of Reintegration Facility into the community, e.g. doctor's appointment, job search, etc., the Resident will need to fill out the appropriate request form at least 24 hours prior in order for transportation to be arranged, unless notified otherwise by staff.
	12. While in the presence of children or teenagers, Residents will not attempt to form relationships.
	13. Residents will not initiate or facilitate social interactions that could result in risky situations. A risky situation is defined as a

	situation that is therapeutically contra-indicated and/or contrary to their treatment plan or relapse prevention plan. For example, talking to a child while at the library.
	14. On-premises visitors may be allowed when a Resident is on the appropriate step, subject to approval by the Reintegration Facility Treatment Team, and will require at least 48 hours notice, unless notified otherwise. All visitors must be at least 18 years of age. Residents will still be required to pick up the phone when called or appear in person when checked on.
	15. All Reintegration Facilities are non-smoking.
	16. No alcohol, illicit drugs, pornography or weapons will be allowed on a Resident's person or on Reintegration Facility property at any time.
	17. Residents will be supervised via monitoring and video surveillance system. Residents

	will at no time touch or place anything on or over any alarm equipment. This will be considered a major breach of security and serious actions will be taken.
	18. Residents will comply and be cooperative with any searches conducted of their belongings, and if necessary, their person. The staff member conducting the search will define compliance and cooperation as inappropriate or appropriate. This includes but is not limited to attitude, body language and comments.
	19. Residents will clean up after themselves and prepare their own meals. Cleaning up after one's self includes, but is not limited to: washing dishes, laundry, vacuuming, taking out trash and garbage, maintaining appropriate hygiene, and cleaning all areas of the building.
	20. Residents will not enter any bedroom other than their own without prior authorization

	from staff. Residents must stand outside the bedroom door to talk to another Resident. Residents will not linger outside another bedroom. Lingering is defined as more than a few seconds. Residents will not be allowed to enter another bedroom unless staff has authorized the visit.
	21. Residents will at no time procure or participate in services of a sexual nature, including but not limited to phone sex lines, sexually oriented chat rooms, live sex services and sexually oriented conversations.
	22. Residents will be respectful of others boundaries and refrain from horseplay.

Violations of RF rules and directives may result in a loss of privileges or return to LSH campus. Repeated or extreme violations may result in disciplinary action such as return to the LSH campus and/or legal charges.

Rule Violation and Sanction Guidelines

Pre-Release: Reintegration

The treatment team will be responsible for identifying appropriate sanctions for rule infractions at the reintegration facility. The sanction imposed should be proportionate to the infraction. In the event that similar rule infractions occur by the same Resident multiple times the sanction should be greater than the one before or additional restrictions placed on the Resident. In the event that a Resident has multiple infractions that are interrelated the sanction(s) imposed could be more severe to match the level of risk.

All rule violations issued will be used in consideration for advancement through the step levels regardless of sanctions issued or not issued. All violations and sanctions are provided to the individual and group therapist for review and discussion in session.

Typical length of restriction or reductions is dependent upon the severity level of the infraction(s). Low severity level infractions typically do not have lengths of restriction unless the Resident has demonstrated a pattern of failure to follow the rule. Medium security level infractions will have lengths of restrictions between 10 days and up to 60 days depending on the particular rule violation and associated level of risk.

Medium security level infractions that do not pose an increased risk to the community, such as failing to document phone calls made or received, would receive a restriction at the lower end of the bar. Medium security level infractions that would increase the risk to the community, such as failing to check in from pass as required, would receive a restriction towards the top end of the bar. High security level infractions should be handled in the most conservative manner necessary to decrease the risk to the community. High security level infractions should have restrictions of 60 days or greater.

Step Program

Step programs are individualized and based on each residents treatment needs.

Step 1 Part A:

This step is designed to give the Resident time to adjust to his new surroundings and complete some preliminary tasks before beginning community transition. The Resident stays on Part A; until it is completed. Movement to Part B will depend upon the completion of all requirements set forth in Part A.

The Resident must obtain proper identification and keep current said identification throughout placement at the RF. The Resident must also register with the Sheriff Department if applicable. Residents will open a checking account and pay rent monthly. Residents will be given a financial allowance dependent upon their needs. The amount charged for rent will be based on the Resident's financial disclosure and income.

Residents on this stage may only leave the building with a staff member.

Residents on this phase will have few initial privileges. They may be given an allowance and spend it freely on items deemed appropriate by the RF Director. Residents are required to purchase a personal cell phone and can make calls freely. Residents will attend individual and group therapy as scheduled. Residents will be required to maintain an accurate, organized, and up-to-date logbook.

Step 1 Part B:

This step is designed to re-introduce the Resident into the community. The Resident will have one weekly activity in the community. Staff will accompany and participate with the Resident on this activity.

If clinically indicated, the Resident will begin participating in relevant recovery support group(s) in the community.

The Resident will maintain a personal checking and savings account. The Resident will complete a monthly budget. The Resident will pay monthly rent. Both the budget and rent payment are due at the 1st of each month. Rent is determined on a sliding scale.

The Resident will begin looking for employment or other approved activity as recommended by his treatment plan. The Resident must search for employment or other activity until it is obtained and approved by the treatment team. After obtaining employment or other activity, the Resident must maintain a working schedule of 32 or more hours per week for 4 consecutive weeks. Staff provides transportation.

Step 2 Part A:

Step Two is designed to keep the Resident in a steady working environment and include passes on their days off.

Residents are allowed passes on their own. Passes can be revoked at any time staff deem necessary. Residents are eligible for approved pass time on one (1) day off from work a week. Residents will be driven to and from one pass location only. Passes will be at least one hour in duration up to a maximum of four hours in duration. All pass requests must have the approval of Treatment Team. Residents will be allowed to attend a local religious center one time per week.

Resident will attend a minimum of one (1) approved relevant recovery support group in the community as required. Residents will attend individual and group therapy as scheduled. Residents will be required to maintain an accurate, organized, and up-to-date logbook. Residents will be required to maintain a personal checking account, keeping correct balances. Residents will pay rent monthly. The amount charged for rent will be based on the Resident's financial disclosure and income.

Step 2 Part B:

This step is designed to allow the Resident to find and purchase a vehicle or submit an alternative transportation plan. The vehicle must be properly registered and insured.

Pre-Release: Reintegration

The resident will drive self to and from work for a minimum of four weeks. They will keep an accurate mileage log. The resident will complete a weekly itinerary, submitted on Friday by noon for approval for the following week. Residents will begin working on a conditional release plan.

Resident must maintain a working schedule of 32 or more hours per week, continue to build social support and attend appropriate treatment.

Step 3A:

The Resident will drive themselves to all activities, passes and work shift. Itineraries are submitted on Friday mornings and approved by the Director prior to Passes. An RF staff member must approve any changes to the itinerary and revisions will be submitted at the end of the day.

The Resident on this step will submit a final draft of their Conditional Release plan to the Director. The Resident will request approval from the Progress Review Panel to petition for Transitional Release. After approval from the PRP, the resident will petition the court for Transitional Release.

Transitional Release:

Pre-Release: Reintegration

This Step is designed as an intermediate step between transitional and conditional release. The Resident will drive themselves to all activities, passes and work shifts.

Residents will turn in itineraries to RF Director or Designee for approval by Friday morning each week for the following week's activities. Resident's may make changes to their itinerary with approval from RF staff, but must submit those changes to RF Director or Designee at the end of each week.

The Resident will locate suitable, affordable and appropriate housing (KSA 59-29a11). After approval, the Resident will put down a deposit and pay their monthly payment for housing. The Resident will not have to pay rent to the RF while paying rent for their future housing.

The Resident must continue to pass polygraph tests by an approved polygrapher.

The Resident will request approval from the Progress Review Panel to petition for Conditional Release. After approval from the PRP, the resident will petition the court for Conditional Release.

General Guidelines

Sexual Expression:

The primary purpose of RF is to serve as a program for individuals who have demonstrated problems appropriately managing sexual behavior. Those involved with RF believe that until different thoughts, attitudes and behaviors are established, most offenders use different instances of sexual expression as a way to reinforce inappropriate behaviors. As a result of this belief, RF is making the following rules:

1. Statements, questions or conversation concerning any type of sexual behavior should take place in group or individual therapy session. Discussions of this nature outside of those settings will be deemed inappropriate and not following the program.

2. Pictures and written material that are sexual in nature and in the possession of a Resident will be confiscated and reviewed by RF management and the Treatment Team. Consequences for having such material may include return to the treatment portion of the program at the LSH campus or other

Pre-Release: Reintegration

disciplinary action deemed appropriate by RF and the Treatment Team.

3. The following items are not allowed in any area of RF or in the possession of a RF Resident:
   - Any material deemed inappropriate by RF staff or material associated with the Resident's pattern of offending, such as pictures, drawings, cards, movies, books, cassette tapes, posters, magazines, etc.
   - Any pornographic material.
   - Any pictures, drawings, etc. that may depict race, age or sex associated with the Residents prior offending.
   - Sexual devices or appliances.
   - NO chat lines, date lines or chat rooms.
   - NO Internet service except for program purposes. This will be conducted one of the RF Resident computers.

4. Some items, which include but are not limited to, movies on DVD, movies on videotape, music on CD's and music on cassette, will be

reviewed for appropriateness on a case-by-case by the RF Director.

5. Any form of masturbation is prohibited in any public area, within view of other Residents or within the view of staff.

6. Residents are not to engage in exhibitionism and/or wear provocative clothing.

Room, Vehicle and Person Searches

Room, vehicle and person searches will be conducted on a random basis. Room searches and/or vehicle searches will be done to promote safety/security within the environment. The consequence, if contraband is found, will be decided upon in accordance with Policies and Procedures of the RF as well as the Policies and Procedures of the SPTP (RF Policy Client 1.7) resident Property may be removed by the RF staff or other authorized personnel if it is deemed inappropriate by staff or to be in violation of the rules of the RF or SPTP.

Staff will respect the sanctity of all release items. It is the Resident's responsibility to identify such items and to show them to staff as required.

Items of contraband include but are not limited to the following:

1. Sexual products, literature, equipment, video and audiotapes, DVD's, CD's.
2. Items connected to the Resident's pattern of offending.
3. Illegal substances, drugs, drug paraphernalia, alcohol.
4. Weapons (firearms, explosives, knives, or any item intended to inflict harm).
5. Computer software and documents which contain sexually related materials or are connected to the Residents pattern of offending.

Property

Residents will be provided with basic living necessities. Provided items belong to the RF and must remain in the suite when any Resident leaves RF. Residents will be allowed to purchase items of this nature when on Transitional. RF Residents will be allowed to purchase items for their living area on a limited basis due to the lack of storage and living space. RF Residents will be responsible for the removal of their belongings from the RF, within thirty (30) days, in the event that they are returned to the community, law enforcement custody or the treatment portion of the SPTP program.

Any items and/or belongings that are purchased by the Resident, given to the Resident by family or friends, items from the worksite, or otherwise come into the Resident's possession; and are brought into the RF will be subject to search. It is the responsibility of all RF Residents to submit item(s) to RF staff upon entry to the building. These items include, but are not limited to; clothing, books, magazines, photos, pictures, drawings, CD's, DVD's, or other electronics. If approved, the item(s) will be reviewed by staff and returned to Resident.

Residents may not possess and blank or copied CDs (CD-Rs, CD-RWs, DVD-Rs, etc.)

Residents are not to alter any state owned property.

Clothing

Residents will be allowed to wear their own clothing while at RF. The clothing must not exhibit any profanity, inappropriate pictures or words. Clothing cannot exhibit any item depicting drugs or alcohol. Any item staff deems provocative or inappropriate will be confiscated and reviewed by the Treatment Team. The Resident may choose to either send out the identified clothing or have it destroyed.

Mail

Residents are allowed to send and receive mail that does not violate any US Postal Regulation or violate any rule of the RF. Residents are not allowed to correspond with persons who are in the custody of the Department of Corrections (DOC).

Residents must gain permission to send or check their mail. All mail must be opened in front of RF staff. Staff must see each piece of mail and its contents. Any material deemed inappropriate by RF staff will be confiscated and given to the Director for further investigation.

Visiting Another RF Resident

Resident visitation between RF houses is <u>not</u> permitted.

Residents will not linger or congregate in or around Resident doorways. Residents will not be allowed to enter another Resident's living area without permission from RF Director or designee. Residents will be able to share meals on special occasions providing that each Resident is included and each Resident contributes to the meal. The Director must approve these occasions prior to the event occurring.

Trading/Borrowing

Residents must have RF staff approval before giving, trading, or borrowing any food or belongings with another Resident. This approval must be documented on a Resident request form by the RF Director prior to any property being exchanged. RF staff is not responsible if the item is lost or broken.

Cleaning

Residents are responsible for cleaning their living area. This includes but is not limited to: vacuuming, dusting, washing laundry, washing and putting away dishes, cleaning toilet, sink, tub, and floors. Residents must take out trash and garbage to the dumpster, keep cabinets, shelves and refrigerator neat and free of trash or garbage. Residents are expected to keep their living areas free of clutter; this includes but is not limited to, boxes of unused paperwork, stacks of newspaper, piles of clothing, etc. cleanliness of a living area will be evaluated during room searches.

Damage to RF items or to the living area will be the Resident's responsibility. Items needing repair are to be brought to the attention of Reintegration Facility Management.

Hygiene

Residents will be required to maintain appropriate hygiene. This includes but is not limited to: daily showers with the use of soap and shampoo, shaved or trimmed facial hair, use of deodorant, clean and well maintained clothing, clean bedding, tooth brushing and combed hair.

Therapy

Residents will attend individual and group therapy sessions, unless counter-therapeutic for resident. Therapy can be provided in person or by tele-video, if needed. Residents are encouraged to attend an approved support group if applicable to treatment needs, on a weekly basis.

Prohibited Contact

RF Residents will not be allowed contact with any former victim while residing at a RF, unless approval has been granted by the Resident's Treatment Team and by the RF Director. This includes contact via mail, email, cell phone, or a third party. This will be considered a serious violation and the Resident may be returned to the SPTP campus at LSH.

Visitation

Residents will not be allowed visitors while on Step 1A. Residents will begin being allowed visitors on Step 1B. A visitor request form must be turned in at least five (5) days in advance.

Visitation is subject to denial by the Treatment Team if a high risk situation is identified as defined in the Resident's Treatment Plan. Visits are to be non-physical and conversation must remain appropriate. There will be no kissing, touching, or other sexual behavior allowed. RF staff may ask a visitor to leave the RF at any time deemed necessary to maintain the safety/security and therapeutic environment.

Residents are responsible for informing their visitors, prior to arriving at the Reintegration Facility, of the rules and necessary information needed. All visits will be monitored by visual and phone checks. All visitors must be <u>at least 18 years of age</u> unless otherwise approved by the Treatment Team on an individual basis. Visits with those individuals under the age of 18 are subject to denial. Such visits will only occur on rare occasions and will not occur with any other Residents aside from the approved Resident. Residents who have a past history of child offending will be <u>denied</u> visitation with children/adolescents.

Property is not to be exchanged during visitation unless prior approval is granted by the Reintegration Facility Director.

Visitors will not be permitted to bring cameras or cell phones in to the RF.

Passes

Residents will not be allowed passes while on the Step 1A or Step 1B. passes begin when the Resident progresses to Step 2. Pass request forms must be turned in at least 72 hours in advance. The form must be filled out correctly and completely. The RF Director will approve or deny any pass. Passes may be revoked at any time deemed necessary.

Residents will not be allowed in any area that children congregate. This includes but is not limited to: toy stores, arcades, clothing store for children, parks, playgrounds, schools, daycares, restaurants with play areas or bus stops. Additional areas are subject to denial by the RF Director (e.g. McDonalds, amusement parks, etc.). some areas may be restricted at specific times at the discretion of the RF Director.

Failure to comply with this rule can result in disciplinary action up to return to the LSH Campus or legal action resulting in revocation of parole.

Activities with Staff

RF Residents on Step 1B will be required to complete an activity with staff once per week. RF staff will accompany the Resident and participate in the activity with the Resident. This activity must be submitted to the RF Director at least 24 hours in advance for approval or denial. Activities with staff should last a minimum of one (1) hour but not exceed four (4) hours. Residents are encouraged to participate in free or inexpensive activities due to the Resident's limited income.

Residents will not be allowed in any area that children congregate. This includes but is not limited to: toy stores, arcades, clothing stores for children, parks, playgrounds, schools, daycares, restaurants with play areas, or bus stops. Additional areas are subject to denial by the Reintegration Facility Director (e.g. McDonalds, amusement parks, etc.) Some areas may be restricted at specific times at the discretion of the RF Director. Failure to comply with this rule can result in disciplinary action such as return to the treatment portion of the program or legal action resulting in revocation of parole.

Religious Services

Residents are encouraged to participate in their chosen religious services while living at the RF.

- Residents on the 1A are allowed to have a religious official provide services at the RF one time per week while.

- Residents on *Step 1B* may attend religious services in the community. Attendance at services can be used as the Activity with Staff or in addition to the Activity with Staff.

- Residents on *Step 2* will be allowed to attend a religious service in the community one time per week. Attendance at a religious service will not be included in the total hours of pass time required.

Due to the total amount of required pass hours, Residents on *Step 3A* may use religious services as pass time to meet the total pass hours required.

Transportation

Residents will be transported to all activities, passes, work, meetings, and appointments by RF staff, as required. Residents must complete a transportation request at least 24 hours in advance. The form must be filled out completely or it will not be approved. Transportation requests do not need to be completed for passes, laundry or any staff scheduled activity. While being transported via RF vehicles, Residents will be required to wear the provided seat belts at all times. RF Residents will be expected to lock all vehicle doors upon exit as well as make sure all windows are closed. RF Residents will be responsible for removing all trash or personal items upon exiting the vehicle.

Cell Phone

Residents must obtain a cell phone prior to advancing to Step 1B. residents must carry the phone at all times. When RF staff calls Residents, the Resident must answer regardless of time or place. When Residents obtain a job, it will be required that they carry the phone on their person unless reasonable accommodations are made in agreement with the employer and the RF Director. Residents must answer the phone while on pass at any time RF staff call. RF Residents are not permitted to call another RF Resident while either Resident is at work. Text messages may be received and sent, however, all received and sent messages must be documented in the Resident's logbook just as a phone call would be documented. Resident will be required to note who the text is to/from, time text was sent/received, and phone number the text was sent to or received from. Text messages can be reviewed by RF staff at any time. Residents will submit their phone bill to the Director of the RF for review. The phone bill must be submitted at the time it is received.

Resident Checks

RF staff will check on Residents throughout the day. Residents must answer the phone when staff calls and be seen when staff come to their suite. Resident checks will be conducted on the RF Residents while Residents are in the community as well.

Log Book:

Residents will be required to complete a daily log book. All phone calls made and received, to/from, and time on/off must be logged in chronological order. Phone calls should be logged including a phone number for each location or person called. Appointments, meetings, visits, shopping, and work must be logged in chronological order. All receipts must be kept and logged in the logbook. Logbooks must be neat, organized and the information must be thorough and up-to-date. RF staff will review logbooks at least monthly for accuracy as deemed necessary based on Residents behavior or failure to document information in the log book. All entries should be made in ink, no white out should be used. All incidental contact with minors shall be noted in the Resident's log book and discussed with their therapist weekly.

Medication

Any Resident prescribed medication will be required to fill out a Medication Administration Record (MAR) daily. This will be turned in to the RF Director on Sunday evening. No illegal or illegally obtained medication will be allowed at RF at any time. The RF will not dispense any medication to RF Residents. RF Residents are expected to understand and be in compliance with their medication needs when they arrive at the RF. RF Residents will obtain their prescription medication through an approved pharmacy. RF Residents will be expected to follow Doctor Orders when received. Residents are required to document all PRN and over the counter medications on the MAR

Note: Medication compliance is an important part of the treatment process and is expected to be followed. Failure to comply with medication may result in being returned to LSH.

Medical Care and Treatment

RF Residents will contact the Director to discuss medical appointments that are needed. RF Residents are responsible for scheduling their medical appointments with the approved primary care physician. RF Residents without medical insurance will submit their statements to the Director for payment. RF Residents that have obtained medical insurance will be responsible for the payment of their medical care and treatment. RF Residents that are on Transitional Release will be responsible for the payment of their medical care and treatment; unless special circumstances exist and must be approved by the SPTP Program Director. RF Residents that have refused to complete a Financial Disclosure Form will be responsible for the payment of their medical care and treatment.

Dental Care and Treatment

RF Residents will contact the Director to discuss dental appointments that are needed. RF Residents are responsible for scheduling their dental appointments as needed with an approved dentist. RF Residents without dental insurance will submit their statements to the Director for payment. RF Residents that have obtained dental insurance will be responsible for the payment of their dental care and treatment. RF Residents that are on Transitional Release will be responsible for the payment of their dental care and treatment; unless special circumstances exist and must be approved by the SPTP Program Director. RF Residents that have refused to complete the Financial Disclosure Form will be responsible for the payment of their dental care and treatment.

Vision Care and Treatment

RF Residents will contact the Director to discuss vision appointments that are needed. RF Residents are responsible for scheduling their vision care appointments with an approved eye doctor. RF Residents without vision insurance will submit their statements to the Director for payment. RF Residents that have obtained vision insurance will be responsible for the payment of their vision care and treatment. RF Residents that are on Transitional Release will be responsible for the payment of their vision care and treatment; unless special circumstances exist and must be approved by the SPTP Program Director. RF Residents that have refused to complete the Financial Disclosure Form will be responsible for the payment of their vision care and treatment.

Parole/Registration

RF Residents are to attend all parole meetings. If a parole meeting needs to be cancelled, the Director must be informed and the meeting rescheduled. Residents are required to notify the Director when the meeting is rescheduled.

RF Residents will need to register with the local Sheriff's Department. This must be completed within the first two weeks of residency at the RF.

Polygraph Examinations

Residents will be subject to routine polygraph examinations. Deception that is indicated on a polygraph examination could result in the Resident being returned to the inpatient treatment portion of the SPTP program on the LSH campus. The presence of treatment violations will be considered a failure.

- Residents on Step 1, 2 and 3A will be financially responsible for all or a portion of the cost of a polygraph if the results of the polygraph indicate.
- Residents on Transitional Release will be financially responsible for the entire cost of any polygraph; regardless of the result unless a financial burden will be created.

Rent, Laundry, and Budgeting

RF Residents will be required to submit monthly rent payments to the Director no later than the first day of the month. Checks should be made payable to "Larned State Hospital" or "Parsons State Hospital" respectively. RF Residents will be required to submit a monthly budget to the Director no later than the first day of the month.

Computer Usage

Residents will be permitted to purchase and/or possess their own personal computers while residing at a RF. The Resident's computer, computer software, computer accessories including floppy disks, flash drives, and CD's will be subject to random searches. All documents created and saved on the computer and computer accessories will be saved in a readable and unprotected form. RF management may request that the Resident open and/or relinquish any computer-generated documents at random and during room searches. Residents will at no time use their computers, cell phones or other electronic devices to access the Internet or save materials considered detrimental to their treatment.

RF Residents will not be permitted to have Internet access on their personal computer. RF Residents have access to the Internet on the Resident computer located in the RF. This computer is to be used for job searching, car searches, and other items deemed necessary for program purposes. RF Residents will not be permitted to play any games on the Resident computer.

RF Residents will be provided with an email account for **job searching purposes only.** RF Residents will **not** be allowed to have any other type of online account or email account. If a RF Resident is found to have one or both of these accounts, disciplinary action may be taken. These types of accounts include but are not limited to: any online cell phone account and email accounts. Residents have access to legal information at their local libraries.

Media Storage

Residents may not possess any blank or copied CDs (CD-Rs, CD-RWs, DVD-Rs, etc.)

Job Searching

Obtaining employment is a focus for each Resident while progressing through the SPTP program. Residents will begin job searching on Step 1B. residents will be required to search for employment by utilizing the Resident computer, local classifieds, WorkForce Center, employment agencies and other resources. Residents will submit potential job sites to the Director for approval. Residents are then transported to all approved locations to submit applications. The Treatment Team at the RF will determine the minimum hours of searching required weekly as well as the minimum number of applications submitted weekly.

RF Residents must present themselves in a professional manner when job searching and interviewing. They are to dress in appropriate attire and the RF Residents must maintain appropriate hygiene. Appropriate attire and hygiene is defined below:

1. RF Residents will be expected to wear khaki style pants, nice jeans or dress slacks.
2. Shirts should be either polo style or button down.
3. Jeans and shirts will be free of tears, holes or stains.
4. Clothing will be free of words or pictures.

5. Residents will not wear shorts, sweatpants, sweatshirts, tank tops, sleeveless shirts or t-shirts.

6. Appropriate footwear such as loafers, dress shoes, boots and nice tennis shoes. Open toed sandals, flip flops or shower shoes are not considered appropriate footwear.

7. RF Residents will be free of body odor, hair will be clean and neatly combed, facial hair trimmed. Fingernails and hands will be clean and nails appropriately trimmed. RF Residents will maintain appropriate dental hygiene.

RF Residents who report for transport to job searching or interviews and are not in compliance with this policy will not be provided transportation to the requested locations.

Resident Grievance(s)

Residents at the RF are provided access to the Resident grievance policy and procedure; Client 1.25: Denial or Restriction of a Resident Right. This policy is located in the Policy and Procedure notebook in the RF lobby where Resident forms are kept.

Note: Residents are to exhaust this internal grievance process ***prior*** to submission of any district court action. K.S.A. § 59-29a24.

Resident Rights

Residents at the RF are provided access to the Denial or Restriction of a Resident Right policy and procedure. This policy is located in the Policy and Procedure notebook in the RF lobby where Resident forms are kept.

Tornado/Severe Weather

RF Residents will be informed of approaching severe weather. All activities off grounds will be cancelled. RF staff will inform the Residents on the actions that are to be taken. In the event that a tornado is in the immediate vicinity, RF Residents are to gather a heavy blanket, coat, or pillow and report to the designated shelter area. Staff will meet Residents in the designated shelter area. Staff and Residents will remain in the designated shelter area until the "all clear" has been given.

Fire Alarm

When a fire alarm sounds, RF Residents are to exit the building immediately. Residents are to report to the predetermined meeting area as outlined in the Fire response policy. RF Residents are not to call staff and ask permission to open their door, try to gather belongings, or wait for staff to call. Staff will meet Residents outside the building at the designated location. RF Residents are expected to have on clothing that covers their body. Shoes are not a necessity.

RF Residents are expected to exit the building in a quick and organized fashion. Exiting the building should take no more than a couple of minutes. **Residents are not to wait on another Resident or wait for staff.** Residents will not be permitted to re-enter the building until the all clear is given.

Chapter 3: The 2018 Version

In August of 2018 the Reintegration facility issued a new rule book. To provide a transparent view of how the facility operates and what one could expect while in reintegration I have included it in its entirety, copied word for word.

Introduction

The Sexual Predator Treatment Program (SPTP) Reintegration Facilities are located at Larned State Hospital (LSH), Osawatomie State Hospital (OSH) and Parsons State Hospital and Training Center (PSHTC). A Reintegration Facility (RF) accepts Residents who the Progress Review Panel (PRP) determined to have satisfied all requirements necessary for transition from the secured SPTP facility at LSH to a less therapeutic setting of a RF.

To be deemed ready for advancement to a RF, Residents must have completed Tiers 1 and 2, be recommended by the clinicians with whom the Resident works, and have shown/demonstrated the motivation to live a life free of crime. Residents must also interview with and be approved by the PRP for advancement.

RF Residents advance through this portion of the Sexual Predator Treatment Program on a Step System that allows an increasing level of freedom to make their own decisions and assist RF Residents adjustment and reintegration into the community. Because the RF is designed to be a less restrictive placement option, Residents are given many responsibilities and privileges; consequently, Residents are expected to follow rules reflective of this unique therapeutic environment.

Furthermore, the RF conditions and expectations are designed to facilitate the Resident's safe reintegration into the community by holding the Resident responsible and accountable for their actions. Throughout this reintegration process, Residents are expected to be respectful, honest, and remain dedicated to their success in the Sexual Predator Treatment Program. The goal is to ensure that while at the RF the resident has acquired the living skills necessary to safely live in the community without reoffending.

Definitions

Contact: Face-to-Face or telephonic communication, written correspondence, physical touching, computer, or any indirect communication through another person or method of communication.

Contraband: 1) Any item, or part of an item, that is inherently capable of causing damage or injury to persons or property, may assist in an escape, or is capable or likely to produce or precipitate dangerous situations or conflict 2) Any item that can be the basis for a charge of a felony and/or misdemeanor for its possession under the laws of Kansas or the United States. 3) Any item that, although authorized, is misused if the item in its misused and/or modified form has the capability of being able to cause damage or injury to persons or property or being likely to precipitate dangerous situations or conflicts. 4) Any item that would constitute a violation of K.S.A. 21-5914 "Traffic in contraband in a correctional institution or care and treatment facility." 5) Any item prohibited pursuant to SPTP or RF rules. 6) Minor-Related material, as defined in this section. 7) Sexual explicit material, as defined in this section. 7) Therapeutically Contraindicative Material, as defined in this section.

Media: Any book, magazine, drawing, painting, writing, picture, movie, video game, item, device, or any similar object containing a visual, verbal, or auditory depiction, or theme.

Minor: Any person under 18 years of age.

Minor-Related Material: Media comprising of minors being in a main primary character role and/or contributing to the plot or are in the intended audience.

Sexual Explicit Material: Any material that has the purpose for sexual arousal or gratification. Material that contains nudity, which shall be defined as the depiction or display of any state of undress in which the (1) human genitals, (2) pubic region, (3) buttock, or (4) female breast at a point below the top of the areola, are less than completely and opaquely covered; or containing any display, actual or simulated, or description of any of the following: (1) sexual intercourse or sodomy, including genital-genital, oral genital, anal-genital, and anal-oral contact, whether between persons of the same or differing gender, (2) masturbation, (3) bestiality, (4) sadomasochistic abuse, or (5) the exploitation of any person. Any material containing inappropriate sexual content including, but not limited to, voyeurism, men/women/children in submissive and/or powerless roles, or men/women/children being abused or demeaned.

<u>Therapeutically Contraindicative Material</u>: Media considered contraindicative to a resident's treatment by the primary treatment facilitator and/or treatment team including, but not limited to, media associated resident's prior offending patterns, material and/or themes that could compromise the safety and security of the facility and/or community, media depicting torture in the form of bondage, dominance, submission, and sexual explicit material.

Conditions

The following conditions are applicable to all Residents at the RF. A Resident's failure to meet these conditions may result in a sanction which can include returning to the secured SPTP facility at LSH. These conditions are intended to establish an environment that is therapeutic in nature designed to facilitate Residents' introduction and transition into less restrictive community-based environment.

1. General

   a. To develop an atmosphere of trust that is expected as Residents transition into a lesser restrictive environment, Residents are to be honest with RF Staff, Therapists, Parole Officer, Lawyers, Doctors and any other agency staff with whom the Residents have contact.

   b. Residents will be respectful of other Residents, RF staff, and to any other person, including co-workers, public, and treatment providers. Physical and/or verbal aggression, which can include arguing (without purpose, reason, uncontrolled, etc.) yelling (in an attempt to intimidate), and name-calling, are not appropriate ways of communicating or solving problems.

   c. Residents will at no time procure or participate in services of a sexual nature, including, but not limited to, phone sex lines, sexually oriented chat rooms, live sex services, sexually oriented conversations, or the purchase of condoms and sex-related devices.

d. Residents will not engage in exhibitionism or masturbate in public or in the view of others.

e. Residents will not engage in any behavior which places the safety of the public or others at risk. To include, but not exclusive of, approaching minors/potential victims, fleeing from staff, or threatening others.

2. Treatment

a. Residents must attend and actively participate in therapy sessions. This includes sharing thoughts, feelings, and descriptions of day-to-day life events. (If a Resident has any questions about this expectation, they should refer to their individualized plans and discuss questions with their therapist.)

b. Residents will follow the recommendations of their therapist and/or treatment team. This includes their individualized Relapse Prevention and

Pre-Release: Reintegration

Multidisciplinary Sexual Offender Treatment plans.

c. Residents must demonstrate attitudes that facilitate rather than deter the treatment change process. Attitudes facilitating the treatment change process include being open and transparent, asking questions, using active listening, and being open to suggestions for making positive change. Deterring examples include, but are not limited to, omitting information, lying, being deceitful, or using derogatory or demeaning language.

3. Supervision

a. Residents will be supervised using staff in-person monitoring and video surveillance. Residents will at no time touch or place anything on or over any alarm or surveillance equipment. This will be considered a major breach of security and serious actions will be taken, which may include a return to the secured SPTP facility at LSH.

b. Residents are expected to immediately follow staff directives. These directives may be given to ensure safety/security of others, to guide Residents out of high-risk situations, or in an attempt to de-escalate a situation.

4. Employment

   a. Depending on their individualized plans, Residents will obtain employment while at the Reintegration Facilities. If a Resident is unable to work, they will be required to participate in approved volunteer work or other approved activities.

   b. While searching and interviewing for employment, Residents will present themselves in a professional manner. Residents are expected to dress in appropriate attire that includes clothing that is clean and free of holes, tears, or stains. Residents will not wear shorts, sweatpants, sweatshirts, tank tops, or sleeveless shirts. Residents will also maintain appropriate hygiene that includes being free of odor, trimmed facial hair and nails, hair that is clean and combed, and daily dental hygiene. The Treatment Team will determine the minimum hours of job searching a week and must approve any potential job opportunity before the Resident accepts and employment offer.

c. Residents are expected to attend work regularly and to be on time for their scheduled shift. Any days that are to be missed **must** be cleared through the RF Director or designee and the Resident's employer. If Residents are not able to attend work, they are expected to contact their employer before the beginning of their assigned shift. Residents must also be approved by the Treatment Team to resign from their employment prior to submitting their resignation notice.

d. Residents are expected to follow their Resident Employment Agreement and policies and procedures of their employer.

5. Contraband/Inappropriate Material

Pre-Release: Reintegration

a. Residents will not possess, hold, sell, transfer, receive, control, or distribute any material that is considered contraband.

b. Residents will not have media that staff are unable to review (ex. Corrupt or unreadable data on a floppy disk, flash drive, etc.), that is considered writable or recordable media, password protected, or encrypted.

c. Residents will not be allowed to have alcohol, illegal drugs, or illegally obtained drugs on their person or on RF property at any time. Residents are also not allowed to have tobacco products inside the RF and will not consume tobacco products while on state hospital grounds.

d. Residents will not have any recording device, binoculars, cameras, electronic transmitters or any electronic device with wireless or LAN internet connections or capabilities.

6. Accountability

a. Residents will be required to complete a daily logbook. All off-ground destinations must be logged in chronological order. All receipts must be kept and logged in the log book. Log books must be neat, organized and the information must be thorough and up-to-date. All entries should be made in ink and no white out should be used. Any correction must be shown by a single line through the incorrect entry and the correct entry added next to the lined-out entry. Any contact, whether direct or incidental, with minors or potential victims shall be noted in the Resident's log book and discussed with their therapist weekly. RF staff will review log books at least monthly for accuracy.

b. Residents will purchase a cell phone that does not have internet accessibility or a functional camera and have it on their person or near them at all times. Residents are expected to answer or make calls with RF staff throughout the day to ensure accountability. When required to call and check-in, Residents must talk with a staff member and are not allowed to leave a message. The cell phone number will be given to staff and made part of Residents' personal information maintained by the RF.

c. Prior to any phone communication with a person or entity, Residents must receive approval from the RF Director or designee. Any unapproved or unexpected communication must be recorded in the Resident's log book and disclosed to RF staff. The call information includes the name, telephone number, date of the call, time of call, duration of the call, and the reason or the call. Any picture message sent/received will also be documented in the Resident's log book and immediately disclosed to staff. Staff must sign off in the log book that the picture message was seen and is appropriate. If the picture violates RF conditions, the Resident's individualized plan, or is not immediately disclosed, it will be reviewed by RF Director or designee and could result in disciplinary action.

d. Residents will submit their phone bill and log book to RF staff for review. These items must be submitted monthly at the time the phone bill is received.

e. Cell phones are subject to inspection by RF staff at any time.

f. Residents will be accountable for their whereabouts at all times. Any deviation from their approved route, itinerary, transportation or pass request must be approved in advance by RF staff.

7. Budgeting and Rent

a. Residents will complete a financial disclosure form and update this form annually or when the Resident's economic status changes (ex. Inheritance, loss of job, etc.). Residents must disclose any and all personal assets currently in their name or held jointly with one or more individuals that they acquired prior to or after their admission to the SPTP.

b. Residents will submit monthly rent payments to the Director no later than the first day of each month. Checks should be made payable to "Larned State Hospital" or "Parsons State Hospital and Training Center" respectively. Residents will also be required to submit a monthly budget, along with all receipts, pay stubs, bank statements, and credit card statements to the Director or designee no later than the first of each month.

8. Property

   a. Residents will be provided a bed, mattress, desk, chair, dresser, and lamp. The provided items belong to the RF and must remain in the room when a Resident leaves the facility. Residents are responsible to care and maintain state property in their possession.

   b. Residents are responsible to pay for the replacement or repair of state property damaged by the Resident.

   c. Residents are allowed to purchase basic necessities while at the RF. Basic necessities include, but are not limited to, food, hygiene items, additional clothing, additional bedding and towels.

Residents will request approval from the Director or designee to purchase any item not considered a basic necessity. These items include, but are not limited to, media playing devices, vehicle, furniture, etc.

d. Residents are required to keep an updated inventory sheet of their property to assist with accountability. This inventory sheet must include serial numbers, brand names, and models of all electronics. RF staff may request the inventory sheet to verify a resident's property.

e. Residents are required to have RF staff approval before any property can be given, received, traded, or borrowed. *Note-This does not include food items.*

9. Searches

a. Residents will comply and be cooperative with all searches conducted by RF staff or law enforcement.

b. Random searches of the Resident's property and person will be conducted to promote safety/security and to ensure the Resident does not possess any material that is considered contraband.

10. Off-Grounds Travel/Transportation

   a. Residents will attend all appointments. This includes appointments that the Residents schedule for themselves, therapy appointments, parole, support groups and any other appointment that RF staff have scheduled for the Resident. Residents must receive prior approval from RF staff before canceling any scheduled appointment. The Resident is expected to reschedule any required appointment at the earliest available date and time.

   b. Residents will be required to schedule activities in the community. These activities may vary in duration and are outlined in the Resident Step Agreements. Residents will not be allowed to participate in activities that are considered high-risk situations. High-risk situations include, but are not limited to, times/places related to the resident's pattern of offending, places where minors congregate, restaurants that are child-themed or have an indoor playground, recreational areas with swimming or boating areas, or crowded or busy times, such as normal meal times at restaurants (ex. 1100-1300 and 1700-1900) and holiday weekends for recreational areas. *Note-When school is <u>not</u> in session, residents should only go in libraries to drop off books and check out another book unless there are clear areas where minors/potential victims are not likely to be present and the time is appropriate.*

c. Residents must have prior approval from RF Director or designee before traveling to any destination off facility grounds. Requests and itineraries, along with maps and activity logs, for all off ground activities must be submitted 5 days in advance for proper review. While off grounds, Residents shall follow their approval requests, itineraries, and Pass Agreements. *Note-Exceptions for submitting required documentation for the 5 day advance will be considered for medical and job searching activities. Residents shall obtain RF Director or designee's approval before deviating from an approval off-ground outing/trip.*

d. Residents that do not have the ability, financial or physical, or are not approved to purchase a vehicle, as outlined in the Resident Step Agreement, will be transported to all off-ground destinations by RF staff. While being transported via RF vehicles, Residents will be required to wear seat belts at all times. Residents will be expected to lock all vehicle doors upon exits as well as make sure all windows are closed. Residents will be responsible for removing all trash or personal items upon exiting the vehicle. Residents who obtain services from the VA medical centers or clinics and receive travel expense reimbursement will be required to reimburse the RF for travel to VA appointments.

e. Residents that are approved to purchase a vehicle will be required to drive to destinations outlined in the Resident Step Agreement. Residents must follow the Driving Agreement and approved routes at all times.

11. Computers

    a. Residents will be permitted to purchase and/or possess their own personal computer while residing at a RF. The Resident's computer, computer software, computer accessories including floppy disks, flash drives, and CD's will be subject to random searches. All documents created and saved on the computer and computer accessories will be saved in a readable and unprotected form. Residents will at no times access the Internet or use their computer to engage in activities that violate any RF condition or their individualized plans.

    b. Residents will only be allowed to access the internet while using the designated Resident computer located in the RF. This computer is to be used for searches related to employment, vehicles, housing, and other items deemed necessary for program purposes. The Resident must receive approval from the RF Director or designee before accessing any website or completing any other activity not listed above.

c. Residents are allowed 1 ½ hours per approved session on the RF Resident computer, unless otherwise approved by Director or designee. Residents will be required to complete a Resident Internet Record for each session of use. Residents will provide the start time, each website visited and the end time of their session. Residents will turn in the Resident Internet Record to staff upon completion of an approved computer session.

d. Residents will be monitored by security surveillance equipment and security software. Residents will not be allowed to access the security software or make setting changes. Incidents involving this type of activity will be considered a serious breach of security. Residents are also required to notify staff immediately when a message box or security alert pops up. Residents will <u>not</u> click on or cancel any message or security alert.

   e. Residents will be provided with an email account for **approved activities** (ex. Communicating with approved contacts for employment, housing, or medical appointments). Residents will <u>not</u> be allowed to have any other type of online account or email account. These types of accounts include, but are not limited to, any unapproved cell phone account, Hotmail or Yahoo email account, and any social networking account such as Facebook or Twitter.

12. Health Care

   a. Residents will contact the Director or designee to discuss medical/dental/vision/psychiatric appointments. Residents are responsible for scheduling their appointments with an approved provider. Residents without insurance must submit all medical information and statements to the Director or designee to ensure proper payment. Residents that have obtained insurance will be responsible for the payment of their health care and treatment. Residents that are on Transitional Release will be responsible for the payment of their health care and treatment; unless special circumstances (ex. Financial hardship, worker compensation, etc.) exist and must be approved by the SPTP Program Director. Residents that refuse insurance, fail to complete a Financial Disclosure Form, or refuse to submit medical documentation or statements will be responsible for the payment of their health care and treatment.

b. Residents are required to provide the Director or designee a list of current medication. This list shall immediately be updated and resubmitted anytime there is a change of in dosage or medication. Any changes need to be turned in same day. No illegal or illegally obtained medication will be allowed at the RF at any time. The RF will not dispense any medication to Residents. Residents are expected to understand and be in compliance with their medication needs when they arrive at the RF.

Residents will obtain their prescription medication through an approved pharmacy and are expected to follow doctors orders when received.

13. Visitation

   a. Residents must turn in a request for visitation at least five (5) business days in advance of the expected visitation. The request must include the name, DOB, contact number, and visitor's relationship to the Resident along with the purpose and plan for the visit. The visitation request is subject to denial by the Treatment Team if there is a safety/security or therapeutic concern. Visits are to be non-physical and conversation must remain appropriate. Residents are allowed to have an embrace at the beginning and end of the visit. "Embrace" equates to a brief hug. The visit will be terminated if physical contact is excessive. There will be no kissing, toughing, or other sexualized behavior, whether actual or simulated.

   b. Residents are responsible for informing visitors, prior to arriving at the RF, of the rules and what

Pre-Release: Reintegration

personal information will be required form the visitor. Visitors must provide valid identification before the visit begins and they will not be permitted to bring cameras or cell phones in to the Reintegration Facilities. RF staff may ask a visitor to leave the RF at any time when staff deem it necessary to maintain the safety/security and therapeutic environment.

c. All visits will be monitored by phone checks, in-person monitoring, and video surveillance. All visitors must be <u>at least 18 years of age.</u>

d. Property is not to be exchanged during visitation unless prior approval is granted by the RF Director or designee.

14. Miscellaneous

a. Residents will comply with registration requirements pursuant to Kansas Offender Registration Act, K.S.A. 22-4901, et seq.

b. Residents will comply, if applicable, with all parole requirements. If a parole meeting is cancelled, the

Pre-Release: Reintegration

Director or designee must be informed and the meeting rescheduled.

c. Residents will be required to open each piece of mail in front of a RF staff unless on Transitional Release. Any items that are considered contraband, minor-related, sexually explicit, or therapeutically contraindicated will be confiscated and reviewed by the RF Director or designee to determine if possession of an item warrants a sanction, which may include returning to the secured SPTP facility at Larned State Hospital or referral to law enforcement.

d. Residents will not consume, possess, or purchase alcohol, illegal drugs, or any illegally obtained drugs. Residents who display behavior, signs or symptoms that lead to a reasonable suspicion of being under the influence of intoxicants or other substances that diminish mental and physical abilities will be referred for a substance abuse screening by the Treatment Team. The Resident will be responsible for the initial cost of the screening and will remain responsible for the costs of treatment and additional testing if the Resident fails the screen. If the Resident passes the screen, the Resident will be reimbursed for the cost of the screening. Refusal to complete the screening will be the same as a failed screening and may subject the Resident to a sanction, which may include returning to the secured SPTP facility at Larned State Hospital.

e. Residents will be subject to routine polygraph examinations. Any disclosure of a treatment violation during the polygraph not previously known by the Treatment Team will be considered a violation. Residents not on Transitional Release will be financially responsible for all of or a portion of the cost of a polygraph if the results of the polygraph indicate a Significant Reaction. Residents on Transitional Release will be financially responsible for the entire cost of any polygraph; regardless of the result unless a financial burden will be created as determined by Treatment Team.

f. Residents shall not leave the State of Kansas or otherwise cross state lines for any reason. A rule violation will be issued if it is determined that a resident has left the State of Kansas or otherwise crossed state lines, even for a short period of time. A rule violation will be issued if it is determined that a resident is actively planning, or has made plans, to leave the State of Kansas or otherwise cross state lines. A rule violation can result in the Resident being transferred back to the secured facility of SPTP at LSH and referral to law enforcement as a violation of conditions of parole, if applicable. RF staff recognize the transition form a secured facility to a RF may cause adjustment difficulties for some residents; therefore, residents are encouraged to contact RF staff for clarification regarding facility conditions and expectations.

General Information

Independent Living:

Residents will be responsible for preparing their own meals and keeping their living areas clean. Residents are encouraged to work together to ensure the cleaning of the common areas are maintained.

Religious Services:

Residents can participate in their chosen religious services while living at the RF. Residents on Step 1A are allowed to have a religious official provide services at the RF one time per week. Residents on Step 1B may attend religious services in the community. Attendance at services can be used as the Activity with Staff or in addition to the Activity with Staff. Residents on Step 2, 3, and Transitional Release will be allowed to attend a religious service in the community at least one time per week. Attendance at a religious service may be included in the total hours of pass time required.

Before Residents participate in community-based religious services, they are required to obtain the written permission from the officiating member of the clergy or other official of the Residents chosen religion. The written permission will be a part of Resident's treatment plan.

Participation in religious services or individual practice of religion is not required to advance through SPTP. The RF recognizes the diversity of belief systems.

Tornado/Severe Weather:

Residents will be informed of approaching severe weather. RF staff will inform the Residents on the actions that are to be taken. In the event that a tornado is in the immediate vicinity, Residents are to gather a heavy blanket, coat or pillow and report to the designated shelter area. Staff will meet Residents in the designated shelter area. Staff and Residents will remain in the designated shelter area until the "all clear" has been given.

Fire Alarm:

When a fire alarm sounds, RF Residents are to exit the building immediately. Staff will meet Residents outside the building at the designated location. Residents are expected to have on clothing that covers their body, including shoes. Residents are not to wait on another Resident or wait for staff. Residents will not be permitted to re-enter the building until the all clear is given.

Residents are expected to become acquainted with the location of fire exits that are identified on the emergency exit chart on the walls throughout the RF.

Severe weather and fire alarm drills will be scheduled throughout the year.

Resident Allowance Information

Rent is due the first day of the month unless the first of the month falls on a weekend. If on a weekend, payment plans will be made ahead of time with Residents.

The allowance stipend per month is based on Resident income received before allowance monies are figured in.

If a Resident qualifies for Vision Card/Food Assistance, it is expected that the Resident will participate in that program.

Residents who receive an allowance from the supervising agency cannot purchase

- Lottery tickets of any kind or participate in any type of gambling activity;

- Tobacco products, lighters, chewing tobacco, cigarettes, electronic cigarettes, alcohol or other paraphernalia associated with the use of tobacco and alcohol;
- Media items; such as DVD's, CD's, movies or magazines.

Note: *Income is consider anything of tangible value which includes, but not limited to wages; monetary gifts; royalties; dividends; income received from the sale of any investment, including stocks, bonds, and business interest; any government assistance, to include food and income assistance; amount received from retirement plans, etc.*

Re-Integration Facility

Income/Allowance/Rent Chart

Income Per Month	Allowance	Rent Per Day	Max. Rent
($300 or less)	$220.00	$3.00	$93.00
($301-$400)	$96.00	$4.00	$124.00
($401-$500)	$65.00	$5.00	$155.00
($501-$600)	$34.00	$6.00	$186.00
($601-$700)	$0.00	$7.00	$217.00
($701-$800)	$0.00	$8.00	$248.00
($801-$900)	$0.00	$10.00	$310.00
($901-$1000)	$0.00	$12.00	$372.00
($1000 or more)	$0.00	$14.00	$434.00

Disciplinary Process

Chapter 1: Introduction

In society order is necessary lest chaos ensues. For this reason there are tasks and systems in place to provide consequences for violating the rules of society or the community one is in. This is regularly cited or known as discipline. As with every facet of society, the disciplinarian can abuse their power. To prevent the abuse a process known as due process is utilized. At a minimum due process requires notice, hearing, and an impartial review.

I spent eighteen years in Secure Confinement before going to Reintegration. During those years I only received about three disciplinary notifications. The opposite was true in Reintegration, to the point I felt they were happy to just issue disciplinary notifications. I know your first thought might be: "Well maybe he hadn't changed." I would respond with that could be true if one does not know the facts.

In Reintegration they do use a disciplinary system, but it severely lacks in providing any form or manner of the protection a proper due process system would afford. First, I will list all of the disciplinary notices I received. Second, I will discuss each due process protection afforded for these disciplinary notices.

Chapter 2: Notifications Received

To be factual one must list the issues without alteration or change. For this reason I will include herein a copy of the notifications I received in Reintegration, meticulously copied word for word.

June 21, 2018

The charge was written as: "Dustin failed to avoid media on his TV, in his room, and failed to make an effort to change the channel, with staff present."

I responded as follows: "I cannot be certain if this occurred for I was in bed. I may have fallen asleep with the TV on. Also, I cannot immediately change my channel, it takes 10-30 seconds to change once I locate the remote. In either case the responsibility falls on me and to correct this I have decided to no longer watch television in my room."

The Director issued the consequence as follows: "Thank you for your response and taking responsibility. Please make sure that you are following your Relapse Prevention Plan and the rules at all times. There will be no sanctions given for this violation. Further violations of this nature will result in sanctions being given."

July 11, 2018

The charge was written as: "Dustin failed to avoid PV's that were near the edge of the road at the business parking lot. They were waving cardboard signs. Dustin was facing directly at them and did not turn away from the left hand side of the road until after passing their location. He appeared to be awake, but when asked about the incident while filling out his activity log he claimed that he didn't see them 'I may have been asleep, I have a condition that makes me go to sleep quickly and wake back up.'"

I responded as follows: "This write up is for failure to avoid PV's while riding in a vehicle. The staff reports that there were PV's waving signs on the side of the road and I was facing directly at them. The staff admits they are uncertain whether or not I was awake. They also cite to RPP Pg. 3 # 5, this requires me to avoid areas where PV's are likely to be. This occurred when I mapped an appropriate route. I would like to make it known that any vehicle trip over thirty minutes I am asleep, as documented well in Larned due to a sleep disorder they could not diagnose because they couldn't afford the test. Either way this is a he said he said incident. I will proactively purchase a sleep mask and wear it on any road trip more than 20 or 30 minutes so there can be no question of whether or not I am looking, asleep, or otherwise inappropriately looking at something. I can honestly say I do not remember seeing any children waving signs."

The Director issued the consequence as follows: "See response on rule violation for 7-20-18."

July 11, 2018

The charge was written as: "Dustin failed to avoid the Marmaton Valley Schools visible from both US 54 and US 59 while driving by them. Dustin was aware that the route we were driving had the schools on it and made the comment 'there's the high school.' At no time did he attempt to avoid looking at the locations."

I responded as follows: "This write up is for failure to avoid places where PV's are likely to be. This occurred because staff deviated from the approved map due to convenience. This route was a denied route because of the school. In addition PV's were not likely to be present as school is not in session and it was after 1900 hours. I did state there is the school and averted my attention. In the end this is a he said he said issue. The only thing I can do is to move forward and ensure that it is clear to staff that I am not looking that way in the future. I would ask that if staff deviate a route they go in a manner that does not entrap a client. For instance using bing.com this route is acceptable with a short jog that would ensure not to pass the school."

The Director issued the consequence as follows: "See response on rule violation for 7-20-18."

July 14, 2018

The charge was written as: "Dustin failed to avoid media on his TV, in his room, and failed to make an effort to change the channel, with staff present."

I responded as follows: "**Facts:** On July 14, 2018 at 2100 Hours I turned off my videogame and looked at channel 32 to see what movie was coming on. While doing this Jerry flung the door open and stood therefore about three minutes and asked me what was on. I stated I didn't know for I was waiting for this movie to end to see what was coming on. On the screen were three adults (2 women and 1 man). Jerry never said he thought there was a kid or for me to change the channel. Jerry left but returned approximately ten minutes later and opened the door quickly to where it slammed against the wall and when he saw the TV was off he loudly shut the door and left. **Statement**: I cannot read minds and if staff believes the person on the screen is not an adult they should give the courtesy to say so. To stand there and do nothing and then write the person up later is frustrating and it also does not allow the client any manner to prove or disprove the alleged violation. I further do not appreciate the constant harassment and write ups I am getting from second shift. I do more trips and TV watching on the day shift, yet have received no negative feedback or write ups. This is a situation again where I can do nothing to prove it did not occur and therefore must assume that staff will be vindicated and I will be punished, even though I feel this is not right. In the future I would ask that staff let a client know that they think it is inappropriate at the time and allow the client to make the right decision. **Resolution:** Do what I can and when second shift is here only have my videogame on and at no time watch television, for I cannot think of anything else to do."

The Director issued the consequence as follows: "See response on rule violation for 7-20-18."

July 19, 2018

The charge was written as: "While at Eyecare Associates 2 PV's came into the business. This writer seen Dustin turn to look to see who came into the door, when he seen it was minors he immediately turned his back to the minors. As the minors finished and was leaving the business, the writer seen Dustin turn his body and head and proceeded to look and stare toward the kids as though he was seeing if they were leaving."

I responded as follows: "**Facts:** I saw two PV's come in and did turn away from them. When they left I quickly turned to see if they actually left. I am accused of staring at them. **Rational Response:** This yet another he said she said incident. I now see this further progressed into the beginning stages of my anger cycle. Either way this write up is a notification of what not to do in the future. I will use this as a learning tool and follow the now known rules. Thank you for enlightening and I will change in the future."

The Director issued the consequence as follows: "See response on rule violation for 7-20-18."

July 19, 2018

The charge was written as: "This writer was in Hallway and overheard Dustin being argumentative with staff."

I responded as follows: "**Facts:** I was arguing with staff because I said something to myself out loud and she informed me that I was not allowed to speak in a public area. I became quite upset and questioned where this authority came from. **Rational Response:** At the time this occurred I was in the beginning stages of my anger cycle and I had no right to argue, in fact this only furthers the anger cycle. In the future I will work on doing as told and not argue. The best I can do is to work on the issue further. Thank you for this realization, through a write up that allows me to rationally see the issue and move forward in progress of my anger management."

The Director issued the consequence as follows: "Per the discussion the Director and staff had with you on 7-19-18, you did not indicate that you said something out loud to yourself and were told not to speak in a public area. You reported that you were upset because staff told you that you did not avoid minors in the doctor's office. You reported that you were upset and got up to walk away. That is when staff directed you to sit down as she was not finished speaking with you. Per our discussion on 7-19-18 you were informed that you needed to speak with your therapist and perhaps needed to attend and anger management course if you became so angry during a discussion on avoiding potential victims that you raised your voice and attempted to leave the conversation with staff. It is not acceptable to raise your voice and yell when you disagree with information being given to you. You need to find appropriate ways to convey your concerns and questions that do not involve exiting a conversation in an angry/rude manner and do not involve yelling. You need to speak to your therapist regarding this situation and work with him to locate and complete an anger management course. Please discuss with your therapist during your next scheduled session."

July 20, 2018

The charge was written as: "Dustin was looking at media (Billboard) on the side of the road that pictured children with adults."

I responded as follows: "On the date in question while driving back from Independence. Staff member Bill told me I missed a billboard with a PV on it. I asked where and he said it was outside the driver side window. I stated I was not looking that way and he said he could not tell. I do not look out the driver side window, for I have enough to dodge in my frontal and side viewpoint. Further, we passed said sign on the way there and I did not look at it. This is the situation where, in writing, I asked Stacey and Brad if I could be held responsible for items outside the driver side window. I have received no response. This is again an indefensible position for me. In fact the writer fails to mention it was outside his window across a few lanes of traffic and a ditch. The simple answer is there were and is no billboards on my side of Highway 169 heading North. I do not look out the driver's side window for I have enough to pay attention to out my window.

My answer to this is I don't know what to say and it is hard for me to accept this when even if there was a billboard on that side with PV's it would have been hard for me to even see it. At this point I am left with accepting what you wish to give me for a consequence, so please let me know what it is so I can properly plan and move on. Thank you for also letting me know I have to have visual out both sides of a moving vehicle. I will now adjust my field of vision to miss everything on all sides of the vehicle. Thank you."

The Director issued the consequence as follows: "You have had a cluster (5) of rule infractions related to avoiding minors over the past 9 days. Those infractions have occurred while watching television, being transported in the community, and while in the community. Rather than address them all separately, it is perhaps more useful to address them altogether. The number of infractions in such a short time for the same thing seem to indicate that you are not making following your Relapse Prevention Plan a priority. We would like to see this addressed, and addressed quickly. As such, you are receiving a one week sanction from watching television. In addition, since some of these infractions occurred in the community, you are being restricted to the unit for the same one week period (with the exception of being transported to and from work, or to needed medical appointments). It is hoped that you will talk with your therapist about your difficulties, and together develop strategies to better equip you to follow your Relapse Prevention Plan. It is also hoped that you will use this one week period to reflect upon your behavior, and make it a priority to follow your Relapse Prevention Plan in the future."

August 19, 2018

The charge was written as: "Dustin failed to avoid media on his TV, while talking on his cellphone. While staff stood there, he grabbed his remote and started trying to change the channel."

I responded as follows: "On August 19, 2018, I was watching television and the phone rang. While answering the phone staff Robin opened my door, I was turned away from the TV looking at my shoe for the caller was asking my size and type. Robin went to leave and stopped and reopened the door. I asked what and she did not respond, at that time I looked at the TV and saw it switched to having PV's. I immediately looked away and grabbed the remote and changed the channel. My RPP states that I am not to look at PV's on the TV. That is what occurred as I was looking at my shoe when it came on. I only had to look for a quick second to see what staff's issue was and then it was turned. I did speak with Brad and he recommended that I turn the TV off when answering a call. In the end it will not occur again for I unhooked my TV. I do not know what more I could have done in the situation and will await a response from the team reviewing this. Thank you."

The Director issued the consequence as follows: "Failure to avoid minors has been an ongoing issue for you. This is not acceptable for a resident at the Reintegration Facility. You need to focus on this area for immediate correction. It is understood that you have discussed this with your therapist and have taken steps to correct the problem. You reported that you have unhooked your television. Please focus on this area and utilize your avoidance strategies to ensure that you follow your RPP and the media guidelines."

Pre-Release: Reintegration

September 13, 2018

    The charge was written as: "Dustin was scheduled to have an outing to Kansas Crossing Casino on 9-13-18. Dustin did not report ready for transport, inquire about this outing, or turn in any paper work regarding cancellation of this outing. At 1700, staff did a visual and Dustin was sleeping in his bedroom with the door closed. This is a direct violation of Dustin's Relapse prevention plan, as one of his relapse warnings is that he may find reasons to withdraw from healthy social activity. This is also a direct violation Dustin's Relapse Program by failing to maintain a healthy social life with Multiple community Activities."

    I responded as follows: "On September 6, my request to do an outing at the Kansas Crossing Casino was approved. The route approved was to go straight from work in Independence to the casino. The outing was to start at 1655 and end at 1855. On the date of the outing staff picked me up from work and deposited me at Maple rather than the casino. At no time did they state there was an approval for deviation from the map or schedule set for the outing. I arrived in Maple at 1617. Upon arrival at Maple no staff member met me or communicated that approval had been granted to deviate from the approved route or time for the outing. I waited till 1630 then went and took a shower and went to bed. In the past when a deviation was approved staff communicated this to me on the drive back and when I came in the door staff met me and explained it. Based on past experience and knowledge of the current rules I figured it was cancelled and went about closing out the day. Reintegration Facilities Handbook Page 8 § 10 Subsection C makes it clear that I shall not deviate from the approved route, time or manner that the outing is set up. I am frustrated that the only notice I got was a write up. In which no reference is made to having approval to deviate as mandated by the Handbook. As such it could be said to act in the manner the writer suggests, by rule would have been a rule violation in and of itself. As such the best I can say is that I should have communicated better or tried to illicit the information I believe that I was entitled to, for example was there approval granted to deviate. I will accept the outcome of this for it will be a learning experience of what to do in the future. Thank you for your time in reviewing this."

The Director issued the consequence as follows: "It is not staff responsibility to notify you of a leave time. You were dropped off at Maple House after work due to staff needs. You state that you were not aware if approval was given. You did not communicate with staff or seek clarification. You are required to complete recreational passes and activities in the community to ensure a balanced lifestyle. It is your responsibility to know what is going on with your schedule. If something changes and you are unsure, you need to seek clarification. At this time no sanctions will be given. Future violations of this nature will result in sanctions being given."

September 17, 2018

The charge was written as: "Dustin was to check in from work site at least once per shift."

I responded as follows: "I have corrected this."

The Director issued the consequence as follows: "I discussed this situation with you on 9-18-18. It has been made clear in your employment agreement and during our discussion that you are required to check in at least one time per working shift. This is regardless of the length of the shift. It is expected that you will check in with staff each shift. This violation will be used in consideration for advancement to the next Step."

September 17, 2018

The charge was written as: "Dustin is to check in once per shift per employment condition #7. Dustin failed to do so during his shift. This is the second instance this has occurred in a single work day, as Dustin is currently working split shifts."

I responded as follows: "I have corrected this."

The Director issued the consequence as follows: "I discussed this situation with you on 9-18-18. It has been made clear in your employment agreement and during our discussion that you are required to check in at least one time per working shift. This is regardless of the length of the shift. It is expected that you will check in with staff each shift. This violation will be used in consideration for advancement to the next Step."

September 17, 2018

The charge was written as: "During Internet Record Review, this writer observed Dustin checking his g-mail account on 9-16-18. At this time, Dustin was observed going through the folders in his account. Once again, Dustin clicked on the "spam" folder and proceeded to scroll over messages with explicit content. He clicked on a message from "friendlype.com." This message contained an explicit message with sexual references. He then attempted to click "Unsubscribe." This brought up a pornographic website that remains on screen for approximately 4 seconds. Dustin then clicked off the website and deleted items from his spam folder."

I responded as follows: "On September 16, 2018, I was going through my E-Mail and found one I did not recognize. When I clicked on it, I noticed it was junk and was getting ready to close it when I saw a button to unsubscribe. As I have done previously I clicked the unsubscribe button in the hopes of getting the place to quit sending the junk mail. What popped up was an adult site, I immediately closed it. No id did not take the time to find the web address and write it down. Instead I immediately typed up a notice via request form of what occurred and turned it in when I got off the computer. Two days later I receive a write up for allegedly violating several rules. To address this we will go one at a time."

"The first rule is RFH Pg. 9 #11b. in order to violate this rule one must be accessing a website or completing an activity for which they do not have approval. I received permission from the director to access my G-Mail account and read my e-mails. It could be said that it is poor for me to decide I could respond or try to unsubscribe to get junk mail to quit coming in. I do not know what to say. As for this rule I was accessing a website I had approval to be accessing and trying to get inappropriate junk from coming in, therefore do not believe this rule was violated."

"The second rule is a treatment violation, RPP Pg. 3 #9. This part of my RPP requires that I avoid all media that caters to children. I do not believe an adult site caters to children. As such I would say there is no treatment violation here."

"Then we have G.R. #16, #21, #23, #26, and #29. Rule #16 requires that no pornography will be allowed on Reintegration Facility Property at any time. My intent was not to do this rather it was to unsubscribe and prevent this from occurring and when it did not work I immediately exited. I would say that most of the junk mail received is pornographic, so it would be hard to enforce this in a literal sense, that is one where there is no intent to introduce it."

"Rule #21 is that I will at no time procure or participate in services of a sexual nature. The writer states that was the purpose of the e-mail and I was clicking the button to ensure they quit trying to illicit me into it by clicking unsubscribe. This shows I was trying not to procure or participate as the rules states and requires. I am uncertain of how this could even apply."

"Rule #23 states that I will follow the recommendation of my therapist. On September 17, 2018, I presented this issue to my therapist Brad Base and he said it seemed like I did all I could by turning it off immediately. I need further information as to how I did not follow the recommendation of my therapist, could you please provide this? Thank you."

"Rule #26 states that I will be honest in all information disclosure. I can partially see this as an issue for I did not list the site that popped up on the internet form. However, as the writer states I immediately closed it once I realized it was improper. I think there would have been more harm to sit and look at the site to determine what site to write down. In addition I did disclose that this occurred in writing after getting off the computer right away, showing I did not know the web site that came up. In one sense I could see your point but also see where I did disclose the information."

"Rule #29 states that I will identify and avoid high risk situations and avoid SUD's. pornography and adult web sites did not play a part of my offending and are not a part of my current high risk situations. I do understand that it can be unhealthy and be a high risk so it should be avoided. My actions show that I was trying to avoid it by unsubscribing from junk that is related to it and in the process was led to a site that I immediately closed, which shows avoidance. As to a SUD I believe this was an important decision for it was meant to get the so called place to quit sending me things than can be a problem."

"After all this discussion I would find that there is a question to determine of whether a person here should have to look at an inappropriate site that unexpectedly comes up to list it on a document, or is it more important that it was immediately closed? If it is more important that it was closed then there be no rule violation, but if the opposite is true I am guilty of not listing the site on the document."

The Director issued the consequence as follows: "You accessed the Spam folder in your Gmail account, hovered over items and viewed captions of what the email contained. You hovered over this particular item and viewed an explicit message with sexual references and then clicked on the message. When you did this additional content brought up a pornographic website. You then clicked unsubscribe."

"The Spam folder is just that. Items that you most likely did not request and are solicitations. If the items are not something you requested you should not be opening them. Just empty the folder. If you didn't subscribe to it, then you don't need to unsubscribe."

"RPP Pg. 3 #9 can be disregarded."

"Please discuss this incident with your therapist during your next scheduled session. You are currently restricted from use of the internet for a period of 30 days for other violations. There will not be any additional violations at this time."

September 18, 2018

The charge was written as: "Dustin is to check in once per shift per employment condition #7. Dustin failed to call and check-in from work on 09/18/2018 between the hours of 07:00 – 12:00."

I responded as follows: "I have corrected this."

The Director issued the consequence as follows: "I discussed this situation with you on 9-18-18. It has been made clear in your employment agreement and during our discussion that you are required to check in at least one time per working shift. This is regardless of the length of the shift. It is expected that you will check in with staff each shift. This violation will be used in consideration for advancement to the next Step."

Pre-Release: Reintegration

September 19, 2018

The charge was written as: "During Internet Record Review, this writer observed Dustin using bing maps to look at Elk City State Park. He clicked a link which directed him to ksoutdoors.com. This website provides information on the park and its facilities. While on this site, PV's remain on screen for approximately 25 seconds in total. Time Stamp 48:36 to 48:54 and 52:15 to 52:22 on Review Video. At no time does Dustin attempt to avoid or scroll away from the images in a timely manner."

I responded as follows: "This notifies me that I have done a poor job of looking at the web page fully. I do not remember seeing any PV's, but again I normally focus on the section I am looking at."

"I was on this website doing research for a task assigned to me by my therapist and the program. I was looking for a place to do an outing and was redirected to ksoutdoors.com to figure out what a trail pass is and how to get one."

"Ultimately if there were pictures an internet record review would not show whether or not I was looking at them or if they were just on the screen. If they were just on the screen then this is no different than being at a restaurant or store where they are and my requirement is to not look. If there is no evidence I was looking at them then there is no rule violation."

"In any sense I will, when computer privileges are returned, look at each page fully and report if there are PV's on the screen, for I do not know what else could be done because they are going to be there, my job is to not look at them."

"I do know with my extensive background in computers that there is a browser setting that turns off all pictures. If this was my computer I would use it so that no pictures would show. However, I am not in control of the computer so I must find another way to access the information. Thank you for notifying me that there are PV's on this site that need to be looked out for and reported."

The Director issued the consequence as follows: "You received a 30 day restriction from the resident computer for previous violations concerning similar situations on the resident computer. No additional sanctions will be given at this time. You continue to be restricted from the resident computer for the duration of the 30 day restriction in place. These rule violations will be used in consideration for advancement to the next step."

September 19, 2018

    The charge was written as: "During Internet Record Review, this writer observed Dustin using a website to lookup event tickets. Immediately a picture of multiple potential victims came up. They remained on screen for approximately 10 seconds in total. Time Stamp 4:42 to 4:52 on Review Video. At no time does Dustin attempt to avoid or scroll away from the images in a timely manner."

    I responded as follows: "On September 18, 2018, I received an E-Mail from PenMac, my current employer, letting me know of a new employee benefit. When I clicked the button it took me to a site where event tickets was what could be earned. I did quickly review the information and closed the site."

    "This again is an interesting situation. An internet record review does not show whether I was looking at the PV's or if they are just on the screen. If they are just on the screen then this is no different than being at a restaurant or store where they are and my requirement is not to look. If there is no evidence I was looking at them then there is no violation RPP Pg. 3 Number 10."

"I do not believe that PenMac SENT ME TO A SITE that caters to children, for you have to be an adult to work with them and earn the benefit. I do not believe RPP Page 3 Number 9 was violated."

"I do know with my extensive background in computers that there is a browser setting that turns off all pictures. If this was my computer I would use it so that no pictures would show. However, I am not in control of the computer so I must find another way to access the information. Thank you for notifying me that there are PV's on this site that need to be looked out for and reported."

"In any sense I will, when computer privileges are returned, look at each page fully and report if there are PV's on the screen, for I do not know what else could be done because they are going to be there, my job is to not look at them."

Pre-Release: Reintegration

The Director issued the consequence as follows: "You received a 30 day restriction from the resident computer for previous violations concerning similar situations on the resident computer. No additional sanctions will be given at this time. You continue to be restricted from the resident computer for the duration of the 30 day restriction in place. These rule violations will be used in consideration for advancement to the next step."

September 19, 2018

The charge was written as: "During Internet Record Review, this writer observed Dustin using bing maps to look at Aunt Mae's coffee and sandwich house. He clicked on a photo which redirected him to multiple images of the place. While looking at these photos, potential victims remain on screen for approximately 43 seconds in total. Time Stamp 41:07 to 41:45 and 41:50 to 41:53 on Review Video. At no time does Dustin attempt to avoid or scroll away from the images in a timely manner. He scrolls over the actual PV twice, the first time taking a couple seconds to scroll away."

I responded as follows: "As the writer notes I was at bing.com, a site approved and required to be used by the facility. As such there is no violation of RFH Pg. 9 Number 11b."

When using bing.com to search a potential outing place I look at the photos, if available, to determine if it is an appropriate place. This means what is the layout and size. When you do this bing leaves the pictures in a small size along the bottom of the screen. This could be why PV's were on the screen."

"The writer notes that I scrolled away from the PV. This is what is required under my RPP. As such I was not looking at PV's and should not be found guilty of violating RPP page 3 Number 10."

"Bing.com is a site that I am required to use by the RF. It is a map site that is not meant to cater to PV's. as such I do not believe that I violated RPP Pg. 3 Number 9."

"I do know with my extensive background in computers that there is a browser setting that turns off all pictures. If this was my computer I would use it so that no pictures would show. However, I am not in control of the computer so I must find another way to access the information. Thank you for notifying me that there are PV's on this site that need to be looked out for and reported."

"In any sense I will, when computer privileges are returned, look at each page fully and report if there are PV's on the screen, for I do not know what else could be done because they are going to be there, my job is to not look at them."

The Director issued the consequence as follows: "You received a 30 day restriction from the resident computer for previous violations concerning similar situations on the resident computer. No additional sanctions will be given at this time. You continue to be restricted from the resident computer for the duration of the 30 day restriction in place. These rule violations will be used in consideration for advancement to the next step."

September 19, 2018

The charge was written as: "During Internet Record Review, this writer observed Dustin using gmail to print off paperwork containing a potential victim. He stared at the

Pre-Release: Reintegration

potential victim for a few seconds, then printed the page off and failed to notify staff of printing the page."

I responded as follows: "The writer states I was using my G-Mail account to review an insurance quote sent to me. As such a violation of RFH Page 9 Number 11b is unsupported as this e-mail account was assigned to me by the facility and I am required to use it."

"This may be my fault for I did not notice a picture included on the e-mail. I will do my best to check for images in my E-Mail from now on."

"A violation of RPP Page 3 Number 9 is not supported for if G-Mail caters to children, I would question why the facility requires me to use it."

"As to General Rule Number 29, I do not know what an E-Mail encloses or has until I open it, therefore, to avoid a high risk situation, is it suggested that I open or read no E-Mail sent to me. I believe that General Rule 29 is unsupported."

"In the future I will do better to look at the contents of the E-Mails I receive and report any inappropriate picture. Thank you for alerting me to this change I need to make."

Pre-Release: Reintegration

The Director issued the consequence as follows: "You received a 30 day restriction from the resident computer for previous violations concerning similar situations on the resident computer. No additional sanctions will be given at this time. You continue to be restricted from the resident computer for the duration of the 30 day restriction in place. These rule violations will be used in consideration for advancement to the next step."

September 19, 2018

The charge was written as: "During Internet Record Review, this writer observed Dustin on fidelity.com. immediately multiple pictures of potential victims came up. They remained on screen for approximately 13 seconds in total. Time Stamp 8:26 to 8:39 on Review Video. At no time does Dustin attempt to avoid or scroll away from the images in a timely manner."

I did not keep a copy of my response to this write up for some reason.

The Director issued the consequence as follows: "You received a 30 day restriction from the resident computer for previous violations concerning similar situations on the resident computer. No additional sanctions will be given at this time. You continue to be restricted from the resident computer for the duration of the 30 day restriction in place. These rule violations will be used in consideration for advancement to the next step."

September 19, 2018

The charge was written as: "During Internet Record Review, this writer observed Dustin using a website to look up life insurance. Immediately a picture of (2) potential victims came up. They remained on screen for approximately 2 minutes and 7 seconds in total. Time Stamp 11:49 to 13:56 on Review Video. At no time does Dustin attempt to avoid or scroll away from the images in a timely manner."

I responded as follows: "I was accessing the site globe life insurance. A site I have been given approval to access. As such a violation of RFH Page 9 Number 11b is not supported."

"Insurance is an activity reserved for adults. I do not believe that a violation of RPP Page 3 Number 9 can be supported, because the site caters to adults not children."

"Ultimately if there were pictures an internet record review would not show if I was looking at the pictures or if it was incidental, they were there but not looked at. If they were just on the screen then this is no different than being at a restaurant or store where they are and my requirement is to not look. If there is no evidence I was looking at them there is no violation of RPP Page 3 Number 10."

"I do know with my extensive background in computers that there is a browser setting that turns off all pictures. If this was my computer I would use it so that no pictures would show. However, I am not in control of the computer so I must find another way to access the information. Thank you for notifying me that there are PV's on this site that need to be looked out for and reported."

"In any sense I will, when computer privileges are returned, look at each page fully and report if there are PV's on the screen, for I do not know what else could be done because they are going to be there, my job is to not look at them."

The Director issued the consequence as follows: "You received a 30 day restriction from the resident computer for previous violations concerning similar situations on the resident computer. No additional sanctions will be given at this time. You continue to be restricted from the resident computer for the duration of the 30 day restriction in place. These rule violations will be used in consideration for advancement to the next step."

September 19, 2018

The charge was written as: "During Internet Record Review, this writer observed Dustin using bank of America. As he was logging on, a potential victim stayed on screen for 26 seconds in total. Time Stamp 3:33 to 3:59 on Review Video. At no time does Dustin attempt to avoid or scroll away from the images in a timely manner."

I responded as follows: "This write up presents an interesting question? What am I supposed to do if a picture of a PV pops up while I am logging onto a website? The writer says I should have scrolled away, but then I could not have logged on to the web site."

"The first issue is that I was accessing a website that I have written approval for to access. As such there is no violation of RFH Pg. 9 Number 11b."

"The second issue is that I do not believe a bank website caters to children. If this were deemed to be true than I would be unable to have a bank account in accords with my RPP. Thus, I believe RPP Pg. 3 Number 9 was not violated."

"Ultimately if there were pictures an internet record review would not show whether or not I was looking at them or if they were just on the screen. If they were just on the screen then this is no different than being at a restaurant or store where they are and my requirement is to not look. If there is no evidence I was looking at them there is no violation of RPP Pg. 3 Number 10."

"I do know with my extensive background in computers that there is a browser setting that turns off all pictures. If this was my computer I would use it so no pictures would show. However, I am not in control of this computer so I must find another way to access this information. Thank you for notifying me that there are PV's on this site that be looked out for and reported."

"In any sense I will, when computer privileges are returned, look at each page full and report if there are PV's on the screen, for I do not know what else could be done because they are going to be there, my job is not to look for them."

The Director issued the consequence as follows: "You received a 30 day restriction from the resident computer for previous violations concerning similar situations on the resident computer. No additional sanctions will be given at this time. You continue to be restricted from the resident computer for the duration of the 30 day restriction in place. These rule violations will be used in consideration for advancement to the next Step."

September 27, 2018

The charge was written as: "Dustin failed to complete and submit his Outing Log for Labette Center for Mental Health, 09/26/2018, within 24 hours."

I responded as follows: "The rule cited by staff is only applicable to clients who are in Step 2a and higher. As I have been denied advancement I remain on 1b. My only requirement is to request the log."

"The writer does not state that I did not request the log only that it was not returned within twenty-four hours. A rule that is inapplicable to a client on step 1b, for when requested staff are to come and work out with the resident/client."

"I cannot say for sure whether I requested the log or not, but it appears that I did for I am being cited for not completing it within twenty-four hours. This would be on the staff for I am allowed to tell staff how and when to do their job. Nor am I in control of this."

"I ask that this rule violation as listed be found improper. As I am uncertain whether I requested the log, I may be guilty of this and for that I am sorry."

The Director issued the consequence as follows: "I will agree that the wording in the memo is confusing. You are required to complete an activity log when you return from your activities. You are to allow 15 minutes for staff to complete office work after returning and then request your activity log. Staff then will then provide it to you to complete. It is due at that time. There are no exceptions to this. Please make sure that you focus on this area so that this does not occur again."

"There will be no sanctions given for this violation. Future violations will result in sanctions being given."

December 13, 2018

The charge was written as: "This writer was doing a computer check on Dustin in the day room. Upon approaching Dustin he said 'what do you want?' which this writer said that was rude and he said he was sorry and was on Golden Plains Bank site. Dustin's demeanor was demanding, impolite and ill-mannered when he made the initial remark."

I responded as follows: "I apologize for this perception. I do not feel that it was demanding or ill-mannered. I understand staff come and check while I am on the computer, and I am fine with that. On this day he stood there awhile, at which point I asked what he wanted. My intent was to make sure there was no issue to be addressed. Again I apologize and will work on this."

The Director issued the consequence as follows: "I am not able to determine if you spoke disrespectfully or not. What I can determine is that you need to ask staff if they want something or not. Staff will let you know if the need to speak with you or need something or not."

"You need to continue to work on the tone of your voice and the way you interact with others. Please address this in your next therapy session with your therapist."

December 21, 2018

The charge was written as: "This writer went in to the day room to inform Dustin that Maple House staff were preparing to perform a room search in his bedroom. This writer requested Dustin's cell phone and wallet, and Dustin informed staff that both items were in his bedroom and not on his person. During the start of the room search, Maple House staff located Dustin's wallet, but could not find his current cell phone in the room. Maple House staff went back in to the day room to ask Dustin where his cell phone was located. And he informed staff he had it in his lunch box. Upon further review of CCTV footage, shortly after this writer informed Dustin of the room search. Dustin pulled his cell phone out of his pocket, and moved to inside of his lunch box, and then from inside of his lunch box to the top of his lunch box. When Maple House staff came to ask him where his cell phone was, he pointed to the top of his lunch box, and informed staff that he had it in his lunch box. Staff searched the phone and found no contraband, and resumed the room search. End of report."

I responded as follows: "On the date in question I returned from work and took a shower. Just after exiting the shower staff approached and stated they were going to perform a room search and asked for my wallet and phone. I stated I thought they were in my room."

"They went and began searching the room. I realized the phone was in my pocket and that cardfolio was in my lunch bag. I placed them in camera range and waited for staff to return. Staff member Jerry, not James the writer of the report, approached me and asked and I said it is on my lunch box."

"In either case I was rushed and made a mistake and stated it was in my room when it was in my lunch pail or in my pocket. I did however make sure it stayed in plain sight of the camera while the search occurred."

"I will work harder in the future to be more prepared for a search and try to make sure to know where my items are at all times. This was not an intentional act on my part."

"Sorry for the issue."

The Director issued the consequence as follows: "I have reviewed your statement and the security surveillance footage. You reported in your statement you made sure that the cell phone stayed in plain sight of the camera while the search occurred. It is clear on the security surveillance footage that you removed the cell phone from your pocket and placed it inside the pocket of your lunch box and zipped it, unzipped it, removed it, and placed it back in the pocket before finally removing it and laying it on top of your lunch box."

"By engaging in that activity and telling staff that it was located in your bedroom makes it appear that you were trying to be deceitful. You are expected to provide items requested to staff when they ask for those items. Lying about their location and then attempting to make it look like they were in another location the entire time is unacceptable and dishonest."

"You failed to be open and honest with the information and items requested during the room search. The sanction given for this violation is that you need to draft a paper detailing the thinking errors you engaged in during this incident and also while writing your response about the incident and why. This paper should be no less than 1 page in length. Observe the margins of the page and do not double space the lines. This is due 1-7-19 at 0800hrs."

This is my response to the sanction imposed by the director: "You request that I discuss my thinking errors. My main thinking error is that while here I would be treated fairly. This issue concerns a matter wherein I mistakenly said something was in my room when it was not. When I noticed this I did not try and hide it but instead admitted it."

"Now I am being treated as though I violated national security. The item was my cell phone. You receive my bill every month on the day I receive it. I do not take it to my room and try to correct any errors in my log as others do. On one occasion I even had to go to great lengths to make sure you have this."

"Personally looking at a phone during room search reveals nothing other than it is the phone I told you I have. On the other hand I receive indifference from staff, lies in writing because of mistakes, and even arriving at work late and receiving disciplinary points from work. Even with this perception I try not let it affect my interactions with staff."

"This is was the first and only time I told staff my phone was somewhere that it was not and yet I sit here doing a lot of paperwork."

"Even though I fell this way and have thinking errors associated with this I do not let it control and create more problems."

"I am to review and determine if thinking errors were involved. Yet, in my opinion am not given an appropriate time frame to do so."

"I received the instruction to do this on Friday after 1700 hours (5PM) and have to turn it in by 0530 hours on Monday."

"Sure I could speak to other residents, but based on past experience they only feed into the negativity. What I mean is they wish to argue staff's improperness. This will not help. In fact the most beneficial person I know of to speak with to make an honest determination or answer is my therapist. However, I do not see one until Monday at 1830 Hours."

"I am therefore left on my own to determine what if any thinking errors were involved. I openly admit I was not truthful with the staff, however it was a mistake that covered nothing and created no harm. As such I cannot determine what may or may not appease your search for what you believe is present that I do not believe may be present."

"I am sorry for the mistake and will do better in the future."

January 22, 24, and 26, 2019

The charge was written as: "Dustin Failed to log the following calls:

Date & Time	Number	Duration in Min	Notes
01/22/2019 1712	Omitted	1	Spam Call
01/24/2019 1537	Omitted	2	Modern Maintenanc
01/26/2019 1650	Omitted	2	Josie's Ristorante

I responded as follows: "On January 24, 2019 I did log the call to Modern Maintenance. In order to show this, please find a copy of my log book page attached hereto."

"On January 26, 2019 I did log the call to Josie's Ristorante. In order to show this, please find a copy of my log book page attached hereto."

"As to the spam call on January 22, 2019 at 17:12 it is not in my log book. However, my log book shows that at that time I was in the common area. A review of the camera could confirm if a call was received and answered. I am uncertain that I answered this call because I have never failed to log a call yet."

"If I did fail to log the call on January 22, 2019, I apologize and will ensure I do not miss one in the future. Thank you."

The Director issued the consequence as follows: "You received the violation for failing to document the phone calls listed in this violation. It is apparent that the copies of the log books provided with your response indicate that the phone numbers are now included. Staff reported that those numbers were not included in your log book when it was received. There is now way to prove or disprove this information at this time. It is expected that you are being truthful in your documentation and not altering the information after a violation is received."

"It is expected that you are documenting phone calls, text, and picture messages according the procedure and guidelines of the program. There will not be any sanctions given for this violation. Future violations of this nature could result in sanctions being given."

February 14, 2019

The charge was written as: "Dustin failed to log the following call(s) properly:

Date & Time	Number	Duration in Min	Notes
02/26/2019 0902	Omitted	2	Spears Mfg. Co.

I responded as follows: "All phone calls in my log book are recorded in the same manner and way. This reviewer is now requiring strict adherence to what is included in the rule book. This has never been required in the nine months I have been here. Now that I know he expects more than previously required I will begin this on March 22, 2019, for I could have not known I was doing anything wrong, based on past action. Thank you for letting me know the new requirements."

"Side Notes: To accurately reflect this incident I believe the date and time of staff knowledge could not have been February 14, 2019. In addition the rule is not on Page 16 of the Resident Handbook for the copy issued to me is only 14 pages long. This does not matter other than to clear the record and record accurately the issue."

The Director issued the consequence as follows: "Dustin, the requirement has always been in place to document all calls properly, the call information includes the name, telephone number, date of the call, time of call, duration of the call and the reason for the call. You continue to be required to follow the rules even if a reviewer doesn't catch the error when reviewing."

"The information cited is correct, however, the previous edition of the resident handbook was cited. The correct edition is the one in your possession dated August

2018. Please refer to page 6 in the Accountability section under part C"

"You are expected to follow the expectations given at all times. Please focus on this area and ensure that you are meeting the requirements."

"There are no sanctions given for this violation. Future violations of this nature will result in sanctions being given."

April 3, 2019

The charge was written as: "During Internet Record Review, this writer observed Dustin using car gurus to look up used cars. While on this site, A PV remain on the screen for approximately 8 seconds in total. Time Stamp 45:15 to 45:23 on Review Video. At no time does Dustin attempt to avoid or scroll away from images in a timely manner."

I responded as follows: "On April 3, 2019, I visited cargurus.com for the first time. Upon opening the site a PV popped up and I scrolled away. At this point I then complied with the rules and looked away from the screen to fill out the Resident Internet Record. It must have been at this time that another PV popped up. A review of the camera would show I was not looking at the screen. Either way it is my responsibility to be more careful. I appreciate letting me know that the first scrolling does not work and I should not fill out the Resident Internet Record until I go to the search screen. I am sorry and will do better next time."

The Director issued the consequence as follows: "Thank you for your response. You are correct, it is your responsibility to be more careful. Even if you scrolled away and completed the Internet record, you would have still had to go back to the screen to close out the page you were on. You should have just gotten off that page to begin with prior to filling out the internet record."

"Please pay closer attention this area and adhere to the rules."

"At this time there will not be any sanctions given. Further violations of this nature will result in sanctions being given."

April 30, 2019

The charge was written as: "Staff AN asked Dustin for his charging station per director. He told the staff no, rang the door bell telling the staff he was going to get it tomorrow, staff informed Dustin director wanted it tonight, Dustin then became argumentative with staff, swearing and yelling, to which director was immediately notified. Director then arrived, to which Dustin became argumentative with her, also swearing and yelling. After 15 minutes, Dustin then complied with staff directive."

I responded as follows: "As the write up shows I allowed to revert back to wanting to challenge rather than not have so much wrapped up in material things. It also clearly shows I put my wants, needs and desires ahead of others and their right to be respected. This is an area I have struggled with for quite some time. However, prior to leaving Larned I let go of the majority of this and sent items to storage and backed off on challenging all decisions."

"As to the facts of this write up the only thing I can do is say that I am sorry and I will again do what I must to prevent any further incidents of this reoccurring. Please accept my apologies."

"For clarity I ask that the radio not being listed as an MP3 player for it is not. It is an XM radio if it was an MP3 player then I could not have had it at Larned. Thank you for your consideration."

The Director issued the consequence as follows: "Thank you for you for your response. You have acknowledged that you have problems with being argumentative and appropriately venting your concerns and frustrations. You have attended anger management classes for this area of concern. It is expected you follow the program rules and voice your concerns appropriately. It is understood that you have discussed this violation with your therapist in session and have been working with him. Please focus on this area for immediate improvement."

"There will be no sanctions given for this violation. Future violations if this nature will result in sanctions being given."

April 30, 2019

The charge was written as: "During a room search, staff AN confiscated an MP3 player per director instruction. Staff removed the MP3 player from the charging stand it was located on. During the review of the MP3 player, MP3 player battery died. Staff then asked Dustin if he had a charger, and he told the staff no."

I responded as follows: "As the write up shows I allowed to revert back to wanting to challenge rather than not have so much wrapped up in material things. It also clearly shows I put my wants, needs and desires ahead of others and their right to be respected. This is an area I have struggled with for quite some time. However, prior to leaving Larned I let go of the majority of this and sent items to storage and backed off on challenging all decisions."

"As to the facts of this write up the only thing I can do is say that I am sorry and I will again do what I must to prevent any further incidents of this reoccurring. Please accept my apologies."

"For clarity I ask that the radio not being listed as an MP3 player for it is not. It is an XM radio if it was an MP3 player then I could not have had it at Larned. Thank you for your consideration."

The Director issued the consequence as follows: "Thank you for you for your response. You have acknowledged that you have problems with being argumentative and appropriately venting your concerns and frustrations. You have attended anger management classes for this area of concern. It is expected you follow the program rules and voice your concerns appropriately. It is understood that you have discussed this violation with your therapist in session and have been working with him. Please focus on this area for immediate improvement."

April 30, 2019

The charge was written as: "During a monthly room search, staff AN confiscated an XM radio from Dustin's room that was found to have contained media that violated his relapse prevention plan and the reintegration facility handbook."

I responded as follows: "Ultimately I have already agreed prior to receipt of the write up that you would not like the music contained therein based on your recent decision. I also asked that the XM be allowed to be sent out. I do not see any further consequences being needed, but if so please see the additional information section for my answer to this."

"In light of this issue I have decided to ultimately send all music out at an appropriate venture. This is because ultimately I would rather not be consquented and/ or have an issue to deal with. I chose to give this up at Larned and sent all items out except my music which was thoroughly vetted and approved."

"Ultimately I accept the decision and wish to send it out. Thank you."

"Additional Information"

"Prior to just accepting any consequence you may to issue I would like to point out several issues with this write up."

"A.   Vagueness"

"There is no information as to the name of the song or artist, to enable one to determine how the music violates the rule listed. Without proper information I cannot decide if it is appropriate or not and the same holds true for the reviewer. Furthermore, most of the music on the radio is the same as the CD's that were approved signed and returned to me. Thus, I have no way to know what we are talking about. The write up form clearly dictates that it is to list the who, what, when, where must be clearly described."

"I cannot even discuss this with my therapist as required due to the lack of information."

"B.   Rules Listed"

"The first rule listed is RFH Pg. #1 Upon turning to page 3 one will find there is no #1. In fact page 3 lists the definitions of different terms used throughout the Handbook. I believe somebody might have used the wrong handbook. Without more information I cannot admit or say whether this was violated."

"The second rule listed is RFH Pg. 5 #5A. This rule concerns possession of contraband. The write up itself lists that no contraband was confiscated. Therefore, how could this rule have been said to be violated."

"The third rule is RPP Pg. 3 #9. In the RPP this states that I will not have media that caters to children or has a theme of abuse towards children. I am unaware of any of my music having this. Further as stated earlier there is no way to determine or answered by me. I can say that most of my music would for sure not cater to children. "

"The fourth and final rule is RPP Pg. 3 #13. This states that I should avoid media playing/acting as children. I am unaware of my music having this. Further as stated earlier there is no way to determine this because the writer did not list the who, what, when, where, and why. This cannot be determined or answered by me. I can say that I know of no music on there where this can said to be true."

"C.   Unlicensed Person."

"In Larned all media was under the same guidelines as here, with one difference a licensed therapy provider did the review. When I left ITU my media was not returned until this occurred including my XM radio. Then a couple years ago it was done again."

"When I came here again my media was seized, but was reviewed by an unlicensed person. This included my XM radio and then was returned to me. I do not see how several licensed doctors or therapy providers were wrong and an unlicensed person with no training, to my knowledge, can make a better decision."

"D.   The decisions of this Facility."

"Upon coming here all my media and XM radio was seized about eleven months ago. After review it was returned to me. This XM substantially did not change since then. Why is it now a problem. Again if the who, what, when, and where was listed this could easily determine if it was done after the review."

"In addition most all songs on my XM are on a CD in my room that was approved, signed off and returned to me. This means I had no way of knowing anything was wrong. If the CD's that are allegedly an issue were listed I could cross reference these to my CD's and show where they were approved leading me to have no knowledge of an issue."

"The back and forth, one day it is ok, and the next it's not. Is unhealthy for me and only leads to further problems. It is apparent to me that one cannot know what is right and wrong based on the inconsistencies of the facility. Thereby, I remove all items."

"E.   Offending Pattern"

"Throughout my fifteen plus years of therapy music has never been listed as a tool to increase, exacerbate or lead to offending. Rather all doctors and therapists have identified my music as a positive tool that allows me to relax and move away from offending both under my anger cycle and my sexual offending cycle."

"Ultimately this decision takes away that tool. As such I have asked that it be removed from my RPP, which leaves a massive void with no replacement."

"F.   The Wait"

"If the XM is now a problem why was it not eleven (11) months ago when I came to the facility and it was inspected? This is unfair to me and my progression in treatment. I operate under the rule that once reviewed and approved I should not then later be consequented for it. Otherwise this is unfair entrapment and baiting."

The Director issued the consequence as follows: "Apologies for the length of time it has taken to review the media items. 76 songs were initially identified as not meeting program rules and/or your Relapse Prevention Plan (RPP). Of those 76 songs, 12 were determined to violate program rules and/or your RPP after final review by the Treatment Team. These songs are listed below:

Little Toy Guns-Carrie Underwood

Pre-Release: Reintegration

When I'm Gone-Eminem

Blown Away-Carrie Underwood

Ms. Jackson-Outcast

Hell is for Children-Pat Benatar

Down With the Sickness-Disturbed

Mother-Danzig

Jesus Take the Wheel-Carrie Underwood

Alyssa Lies-Jason Michael Carol

Mockingbird-Eminem

Temporary Home-Carrie Underwood

I Wanna Love You-Akon"

"Per your request to pack and send out all of your media items, this is approved. The items will remain in the Directors office until you provide packaging to pack and label. At that time staff will meet you with the items and then you can have them mailed out."

May 13, 2019

The charge was written as: "Dustin failed to document in his log book and disclose to staff, a picture message he sent."

I responded as follows: "A few days ago Kimber asked me to explain why this was not logged in my log book and I gave her a response. My response to that was and is the same as I respond here. I received the picture from and approved contact and notified staff and had my log book signed. I then forwarded the picture to another approved contact. I did not log this because I thought once they were approved it did not need to be logged."

"Now I receive the write up. I would note this is the first time I have either received or sent a photo. Based on the write up and my current review of the Resident Handbook, I know that I was wrong and must log any and all receipt or sending of pictures."

"As such I will make sure that even approved numbers are logged if a picture is involved. Thank you for clarifying this and helping me see the right way to handle pictures on my telephone."

The Director issued the consequence as follows: "Thank you for your response. Please make sure that you are documenting calls, texts, and picture messages as required."

"There are no sanctions given for this violation. Future violations if this nature could result in sanctions being given."

May 8, 2019

The charge was written as: "During Internet Record Review, this writer observed Dustin visiting the login screen for Chase credit card. While on this screen, a family with 2 PV's remain on the screen for approximately 19 seconds in total. Time stamp 47:31 to 47:50 on Review Video. This image is unavoidable throughout the login process."

I responded as follows: "In response to this write up I cannot say whether or not this occurred for it was two months ago. Why there is a delay in this I cannot say. In summation I can say that an honest review of the rules listed should not be found to have been violated because they are misplaced or the evidentiary basis is lacking."

"I can say that I do not look at them when they are on the screen as required by my RPP. This is all I can do as I continuously ask them to turn them off and receive no answer."

"I am sorry this occurred again and it seems like it is a recurring issue that cannot be resolved until I can turn the pictures off. In addition please see the rest of the statements herein."

"RFH Pg. 9 #11b"

"This rule states: 'Residents will only be allowed to access the internet while using the designated Resident computer located in the RF. This computer is to be searches related to employment, vehicles, housing, and other items deemed necessary for program purposes. The Resident must receive approval from the RF director or designee before accessing any website or completing any other activity not listed above.'"

"Previously this individual staff wrote several write ups based on this rule and it was found that the rule had not been broken. Again this is the case here, and it appears to me that staff need to be trained."

"First, they state that I was using the designated computer located in the RF. Then at no point is evidence presented that I did not have permission to access chase.com by the Director or designee. In fact the approval was granted on June 20th, 2018, via a resident request form by Stacey Paige."

"I would ask that this individual be provided these documents and necessary training so this continual improper documentation ceases to occur."

"RPP Pg. 3 #10"

"This states: 'I should avoid all media (omitted) that cater to children or have a theme of abuse towards children. I should avoid excessively violent programming.'"

"The term cater is to provide what is wanted or needed in a particular situation to a particular group of people."

"The website was chase.com a bank website. Banks do not cater to PV's in fact they cater to adults, especially a credit card site such as chase.com. There is no evidence of abuse towards PV's in the written part and/or no violent programming."

"This is an improper rule citation for which guilt should not be found for it is misplaced and improper."

"RPP Pg. 3 # 10"

"This states: "I should avoid looking at children, including all forms of media (omitted)." An internet record review is a staff member looking at the videotape of what was on the screen while I was using the RF computer to access the internet. It does not nor could it show where I was looking."

"In fact as stated in the write up it was while I was logging on and it was unavoidable. When I log on I am looking at the desk to read the login ID and password, I am not looking at the screen. This would be visible by the camera pointed at the resident computer."

"I believe and feel this rule citation should be also be dismissed for my finding of guilt would be impractical as the staff did in no manner discern whether I was looking at the image on the screen as required by the way it is worded."

"GR #29"

"This rule states that I must identify and avoid high risk situations and SUD's. Through previous write ups I have recognized the internet is full of images that I must avoid. If this is the high risk situation."

"However, when I have tried to take steps to ensure it does not occur I have received no response from the facility and have not been allowed to turn off the pictures. So to avoid I follow my RPP by not looking at them."

"It is my belief that I have not violated this rule as I did not look at the image. Also, I believe that I continue to be thwarted from following this rule."

"Internet Record Review"

"I have documentation that says an internet record review was completed on April 3, 2019. Why was this not determined then? That is a question that makes me wonder."

"Denial of Method to Prevent Said Write Up"

"In the past I have made it clear that if these continue I need to be allowed to click the button that turns off all pictures while I am on the internet yet, I have been denied this. It is as if the internet is for me to fail and the facility have a reason to continue to write me up and hold me back, months after something occurred."

"Unavoidable"

"The writer states this occurred while logging in and it was unavoidable. A camera review would show that when I was logging in I am paying attention to my book on the desk with the login information rather than the screen. Thus, if it comes up I am in compliance with my Relapse Plan as I am not looking at it."

"If it is unavoidable that is only because I was not allowed to click the no picture button. I do have to log in and did so by not looking at the screen in accords with my Relapse Plan."

The Director issued the consequence as follows: "This continues to be an issue. Use of the resident computer to monitor your credit accounts is a privilege. While you have been given permission to use the resident computer and access the internet for this purpose, you continue to be required to follow your Relapse Prevention Plan and program rules. When reviewing the Internet records you have submitted it is clear that the image remained on the screen for an extended period of time. It is not known whether or not you turned your head away. Even if you had done so you would have returned your eyes to the screen to see if the image remained on the screen you would have viewed the images. You could have closed out of the window. This is the most effective way to avoid the images. When you sign back in and additional images of minors are present you should close out. If these sites continually show images of minors then you should find an alternative ways of monitoring your accounts. This can be done by billing statements and even phone calls."

"This needs to be an area of focus for immediate improvement. This area will continue to be monitored. There will be no sanctions given for this rule violation. Further violations of this nature will result in sanctions being issued."

May 8, 2019

The charge was written as: "During Internet Record review, this writer observed Dustin using Google to look up McCune Farm to Market restaurant. While on this site, a family with PV's remain on screen for approximately 29 seconds in total. Time stamp 23:06 to 23:35 on Review Video. Dustin does attempt to scroll past the large picture as he flips through them. However, the smaller picture on the left side of the screen clearly shows the PV's remaining on the screen."

I responded as follows: "In response to this write up I cannot say whether or not this occurred for it was two months ago. Why there is a delay in this I cannot say. In summation I can say that an honest review of the rules listed should not be found to have been violated because they are misplaced or the evidentiary basis is lacking."

"I can say that I do not look at them when they are on the screen as required by my RPP. This is all I can do as I continuously ask them to turn them off and receive no answer."

"I am sorry this occurred again and it seems like it is a recurring issue that cannot be resolved until I can turn the pictures off. In addition please see the rest of the statements herein."

"RFH Pg. 9 #11b"

This rule states: "Residents will only be allowed to access the internet while using the designated Resident computer located in the RF. This computer is to be searches related to employment, vehicles, housing, and other items deemed necessary for program purposes. The Resident must receive approval from the RF director or designee before accessing any website or completing any other activity not listed above."

"First, they state that I was using the designated computer located in the RF. Then it is stated I was visiting a website concerning a restaurant. This was research towards a possible outing site, a requirement in the program."

"I would ask that this individual be provided these documents and necessary training so this continual improper documentation ceases to occur."

"RPP Pg. 3 #9"

"This states: 'I should avoid all media (omitted) that cater to children or have a theme of abuse towards children. I should avoid excessively violent programming.'"

"The term cater is to provide what is wanted or needed in a particular situation to a particular group of people."

"The website was a restaurant review. Restaurants can, depending on the type, cater to PV's but the name did not appear to cater to this group. There is no evidence of abuse towards PV's in the written part and/or no violent programming."

"This is an improper rule citation for which guilt should not be found for it is misplaced and improper."

"RPP Pg. 3 #10"

"This states: "I should avoid looking at children, including all forms of media (omitted)." An internet record review is a staff member looking at the videotape of what was on the screen while I was using the RF computer to access the internet. It does not nor could it show where I was looking."

"In fact as stated in the write up it was a small picture on the side and I was scrolling past the big picture in the middle with PV's. so my focus was in the middle and not on the side. In fact if it was on the side it appears that it was not an image that could be gotten rid of, so my RPP says do not look at it and I did not look at it."

"I believe and feel this rule citation should be also be dismissed for my finding of guilt would be impractical as the staff did in no manner discern whether I was looking at the image on the screen as required by the way it is worded."

"GR #29"

"This rule states that I must identify and avoid high risk situations and SUD's. Through previous write ups I have recognized the internet is full of images that I must avoid. If this is the high risk situation."

"However, when I have tried to take steps to ensure it does not occur I have received no response from the facility and have not been allowed to turn off the pictures. So to avoid I follow my RPP by not looking at them."

"It is my belief that I have not violated this rule as I did not look at the images. Also, I believe that I continue to be thwarted from following this rule."

"Internet Record Review"

"I have documentation that says an internet record review was completed on April 3, 2019. Why was this not determined then? That is a question that makes me wonder."

The Director issued the consequence as follows: "This continues to be an issue. Use of the resident computer to monitor your credit accounts is a privilege. While you have been given permission to use the resident computer and access the internet for this purpose, you continue to be required to follow your Relapse Prevention Plan and program rules. When reviewing the Internet records you have submitted it is clear that the image remained on the screen for an extended period of time. It is not known whether or not you turned your head away. Even if you had done so you would have returned your eyes to the screen to see if the image remained on the screen you would have viewed the images. You could have closed out of the window. This is the most effective way to avoid the images. When you sign back in and additional images of minors are present you should close out. If these sites continually show images of minors then you should find an alternative ways of monitoring your accounts. This can be done by billing statements and even phone calls."

"This needs to be an area of focus for immediate improvement. This area will continue to be monitored. There will be no sanctions given for this rule violation. Further violations of this nature will result in sanctions being issued."

July 2, 2019

The charge was written as: "This writer knocked on Dustin's door and entered Dustin's room. Dustin was watching and episode of Law and Order SVU about a porn star being raped in college."

I responded as follows: "I do not remember which day it occurred. During a security check by Bill I was in the process of turning my television on. He opened the door and I averted my attention to him before the picture came on. Bill asked me what I was watching and I said I didn't know I just turned it on. As we both looked at the screen I changed the channel and he said that didn't appear appropriate."

"I followed my RPP by changing the channel. In addition to this, Matthew came by less ten minutes later and didn't see me watching it."

"I do not understand why one wishes to accuse someone of watching something when they are there for 5 seconds and I said I just turned it on. Then during a second check, after I agreed and change the channel as my RPP says, it wasn't on."

"Either way I am unhooking my television again to eliminate this problem. I will sit around and do nothing. "

"Thank You"

The Director issued the consequence as follows: "Thank you for your response. If you had indeed just turned on the TV as staff entered the room then you addressed the situation with staff present by turning the channel. It is unknown if you were watching the show prior to staff entering the room, staff go by what is on the screen when they enter the room. Law and Order SVU was on the TV when they came in."

"You have discussed this in session with your therapist. There will be no sanctions given for this violation, however, future violations of this nature could result in sanctions being given."

Chapter 3: Due Process

What Due Process system does Reintegration use for disciplinary write ups? The rules of Reintegration show there is no set procedure, but the rules do show that it will affect one's ability to regain his freedom, the constitutional right of that person.

As there is no process, I will discuss how the process went for each disciplinary notice of a rule violation that I received while in Reintegration.

First, when a staff member believes I violated a rule they would fill out a "Rule Violation Report." This report includes the following information: (1) A statement of whether contraband was confiscated; (2) My name; (3) Date of the alleged violation; (4) Date and time staff became aware of the alleged violation; (5) Location where violation occurred; (6) Statement of the rule violated; (7) A statement of the violation; and (8) A description of the facts showing the rule violation occurred.

Second, I receive a copy. This was delivered via the mailbox. The mailbox is required to be checked once per day by me. It can contain incoming U.S. Mail and any communication from the facility to me. There is no exact method to track completion of service to my knowledge.

Third, I am to put a statement on the form concerning the allegation and turn it back in at a set time. Usually I was informed of the time to turn it in via a sticky note attached to the document. In preparing my responsive statement I am not allowed to see the evidence, speak with the complainant, speak with or get witness statements, and can only use what I have available to provide a response.

Fourth, it now goes to the director. Yes, this is the person that stated to me that staff cannot lie and cannot do any wrong. The director lists the sanctions they are imposing. No, a hearing is not held, I cannot question the writer, review the evidence or any other part of due process. The decision is relayed to me via the mailbox.

This is the end of the process for there is no review beyond the director's decision in accords with the rules. The statute requires that a notice be given and the person be allowed to have review before the Office of Administrative Hearings and then with the Court through a Kansas Judicial

Review Act proceeding. This is set in K.S.A. 59-29a22. For this reason none of the write ups I received in Reintegration have been finalized.

Pre-Release: Reintegration

Paying for Reintegration

Chapter 1: Introduction

As with any state run operation or facility the costs of Reintegration are paid for by the State of Kansas. There are three separate Reintegration programs in Kansas (Osawatomie, Parsons, and Larned). Parsons and Osawatomie receive a separate set of funds from the state for operating the Reintegration house, whereas the Larned Reintegration does not.

According to Kansas Senate Bill (SB) 267 Parsons receives $2,037,289 and Osawatomie receives $1,119,976, for a combined total of $3,157,265. The bill was enacted on May 5, 2022, after the Governor signed it.

Keeping in mind that currently each Reintegration house is limited to sixteen (16) persons, the cost per person is:

Parsons – Cost of $127,330.56 per year, or a total of $348.85 per day per person.

Osawatomie - Cost of $69,998.50 per year, or a total of $199.77 per day per person.

Larned – Indeterminate as it does not have its own budget line.

Pre-Release: Reintegration

The Secretary of KDADS supplements this amount received from the State by enacting the provisions of K.S.A. 59-2006. This law allows for the Secretary to recoup the costs from the person confined. The amount charged is different for one in Reintegration than one in Secure Confinement.

First we will discuss the cost for a person in Reintegration and then show what the cost is for one in Secure Confinement.

Chapter 2: Rent at Reintegration

In Reintegration they include the cost of rent in the rule book. While I was there we operated under two different rule books. However, the amount of rent was not different for either rule book.

Reintegration pays the person an allowance until they earn enough. At the maximum amount of rent collected ($434.00) per month the percentage of the daily rate the person pays is:

Parsons – Four Percent (4%)

Osawatomie – Seven Percent (7%)

Larned – Indeterminate as it does not have its own budget line.

The percentage recouped by the State is really low, but we must keep in mind these men have been in lockup with no funds or job for over ten years. They must start life all over again. This includes buying a house and a car. This should be seen as reasonable.

The chart concerning rent in Reintegration is on the next page.

Re-Integration Facility
Income/Allowance/Rent Chart

Income Per Month	Allowance	Rent Per Day	Max. Rent
($300 or less)	$220.00	$3.00	$93.00
($301-$400)	$96.00	$4.00	$124.00
($401-$500)	$65.00	$5.00	$155.00
($501-$600)	$34.00	$6.00	$186.00
($601-$700)	$0.00	$7.00	$217.00
($701-$800)	$0.00	$8.00	$248.00
($801-$900)	$0.00	$10.00	$310.00
($901-$1000)	$0.00	$12.00	$372.00
($1000 or more)	$0.00	$14.00	$434.00

Chapter 3: Secure Confinement

In Secure Confinement if one gets a facility job they are required to pay rent in accords with K.S.A. 59-2006. The only difference is that they pay more rent than one in Reintegration. To understand this we must look to the method used.

Secure Confinement houses about two-hundred and ninety-seven persons. The budget from the State is $23,242,652 per year (SB 267). This is a cost of $78,258.08 per person per year, or $214.40 per day. This is less than the cost per day at Parsons Reintegration and slightly higher than the cost per day at Osawatomie Reintegration.

In Secure Confinement they are using a formula that was developed in 1995 by a commissioner of an agency that is no longer in existence to determine the rent owed. The formula used is as follows:

((Gross Pay - $127.00)/2)=Rent

In addition to the formula the rent is only taken from the last check for the month if the check does not cover the rent payment owed the facility withholds from the first check of the next month. Using the chart from Reintegration the following would be the rent in Secure Confinement:

Gross Pay	Rent	Allowance
$300	$86.50	$0.00
$400	$136.50	$0.00
$500	$186.50	$0.00
$600	$236.50	$0.00
$700	$286.50	$0.00
$800	$336.50	$0.00
$900	$386.50	$0.00
$1,000	$436.50	$0.00

Unlike Reintegration the amount of rent continues to go up in Secure Confinement for any amount above $1,000.00. We also have to keep in mind the allowance. For example, one who makes $300.00 pays less rent in Reintegration, but then is given a $220.00 allowance. So he actually has $520.00 before paying rent, leaving him with $427.00, in Secure Confinement the person only has $213.50.

It is quite clear that Secure Confinement charges almost double the rent and then leaves the person with only half as much money as they would have had in Reintegration.

Pre-Release: Reintegration

Reintegration is supposed to be where the individual is responsible for the cost of their living as one in free society would be, why is it the opposite? Is it fair to the taxpayers?

As a person in Secure Confinement how can they prepare for the costs of the world when their money is taken? They cannot and this is one of the factors that leads to an extended stay in Secure Confinement and Reintegration at an extensive cost to the taxpayer.

Pre-Release: Reintegration

The Human Workforce

Pre-Release: Reintegration

Chapter 1: Introduction

A normal citizen is expected to have a job and earn money to support themselves. The same is true for one in Reintegration. In fact they expect that the person will have a full time job. There are a few exceptions to this: (1) The person is retired; (2) The person is disabled; or (3) The person has money and desires not to work.

The person has many restrictions placed on what type of work they may do, where they may work, etc. while in Reintegration. We will discuss all of these limits and restrictions herein. We will also discuss what if any preparation is provided in Secure Confinement to help the person be ready for the workforce.

In simplest terms each of the Reintegration houses have a basic place that will hire anyone in the house. This is where most of the people work. I found these to be substandard and low paying and opted to find another job. This caused many struggles and I will discuss some of that in this chapter.

Pre-Release: Reintegration

Chapter 2: Secure Confinement

The first part of treatment in Secure Confinement is called skill acquisition. As having a productive job in the community is a requirement you would think this is a skill they have the person acquire. The sad fact is that it is not something that is taught or acquired while on Tier 1 or Tier 2.

In Secure Confinement having a job within the facility is a privilege. In order to earn this privilege the person must work through the privilege level system. This system has four levels:

A. Gray – New admissions begin here.

B. Blue

C. Green

D. Purple

In order to advance from one level to the next the person must be on the level for ninety days. In order to advance a level, except to purple level, the person must meet the following:

A. Have 90 days with appropriate behavior consistent with the purpose and goals of LSH/SPTP policies.

B. Receive approval of Treatment Team after they review the person to see if they meet the criteria.

C. The person must request review for it is not automatic, i.e. will not be done without the person requesting it.

The almighty purple is the highest level to be attained. This is where the person has an opportunity to have a job, if one is open. To get to this step the person must meet the following:

A. Attend 100% of groups and classes with active participation in the topic and follow all directives of the therapist or leader.

B. Maintain constant program advancement as determined by Treatment Team. The factors for this include: (1) Active participation in group, i.e. provide feedback and present issues; (2) Maintain a transparent lifestyle; (3) Complete and submit RSA's and fantasy logs biweekly; (4) Actively work on and demonstrate behavior consistent with the purpose and goals of LSH/SPTP decreasing maladaptive sexual behaviors, thoughts and fantasies; (5) Actively work on and demonstrate behavior consistent with the purpose and goals of LSH/SPTP decreasing maladaptive criminogenic behaviors and attitudes; (6) Formulate and update Relapse Prevention Plan as directed by therapist or Treatment Team; (7) Attend and actively participate in individual therapy sessions; (8) Actively work towards goals outlined in treatment plan; and (9) Attend to expectations from therapist or Treatment Team.

C. Participate in Comprehensive Integrated Treatment Plan (CITP) meetings.

D. Participate in all assessments, evaluations, or testing to determine the person's treatment needs or risk level (Does not include the annual review examination).

E. Comply with any and all requested paperwork and documents required for outside medical insurance.

F. Comply with any and all requests from Central Information Management (CIM) regarding pictures that must be taken periodically for security purposes.

G. Upon request provide any and all financial documentation related to outside financial institutions and accounts.

H. Upon request provide an updated and accurate inventory of all personal property.

I. Maintain 100% compliance with treatment.

J. Maintain expected hygiene requirements.

K. Ensure room complies with Policy 5.15.

L. Comply with all room inspections.

M. Comply with offender registration requests.

D. Do not display any behaviors inconsistent with the purpose and goals of LSH/SPTP policies.

Once the person has spent the time and achieved all that is required he is granted purple privilege level, which allows for him to have a job. It is true that one must be perfect in order to achieve purple, while the therapists call in all the time and have at best a 60% attendance record. The privilege is hard earned for a limited job spot. It is true that the time the person is on purple he must constantly meet this criteria or he will be removed from purple.

While the committed person served his time in the Department of Corrections, he was assigned a work detail (job) from day one and expected to work at all times while confined. A job was not a privilege in the Department of Corrections. This is important for in the Department of Corrections one is there for punishment but under the KSVPA there is to be no punishment.

Now that we have discussed what the person must do in order to get a job in the facility, let us take a look at the facility job system to see if it can prepare one for work in the real world.

The jobs come in one of two departments: (1) Dietary and (2) Environmental. Dietary is working in the kitchen that feeds all those confined in Secure Confinement. Environmental is janitorial work, cleaning the units. Recently the Dietary department was removed by the administration. It was the largest employment with the most work hours, for this reason we will discuss the environmental jobs.

An environmental job is in essence janitorial work. The person will be assigned to an area to clean for a few days a week. On average the person will have seven hours of work per week. Whether or not they have the skills to do the job, there is no training provided, and they are left with no supervision.

The jobs can and have been abused. Persons log hours of work but never work them, only partially clean, and all other sorts of bad work traits. This in no way prepares the person for work in Reintegration, which is normally a ten or twelve hour shift per day of intense labor. Then if skills are learned as we will see in the next chapter these types of jobs are unavailable to one in Reintegration.

Outside of work the Secure Confinement portion does not have a job skills class on Tier One, where the person is required to acquire skills. Rather the class is on Tier 2, where the task is to be skill demonstration.

In summation one cannot say that Secure Confinement in any way would prepare them for the world of work in society. A very sad fact, that is a vital and necessary skill.

Pre-Release: Reintegration

Chapter 3: Rules

As with everything in Reintegration there are rules for working in the community. Before we look to this, we have to remember that Reintegration would be similar to a halfway house for a convicted sex offender coming out of prison. It will be shown that the job world for one in reintegration is very limited more so than a prisoner faces.

There are so many rules to discuss concerning work that it would be impractical to list them all here. What will be presented are the most prevalent rules. These can be stated as follows:

   A. The job cannot allow anyone under the age of eighteen to be present.
   B. The job must occur in one spot. This means one cannot work at different job sites, which eliminates construction and many other trades.
   C. There must be a supervisor present at all times when the person is at work.
   D. The person may not volunteer or request overtime. All overtime must be mandated by the employer and have approval of the Reintegration staff.

E. The person will carry their cell phone at all times while at work unless the job has rules against it.

F. The person will be required to call in once per shift to check in, even if he only works a shift that is less than an hour.

G. The person is required to take the insurance offered by the job. The exception is if he has private insurance, Veteran's, or some other insurance.

H. The person is required to provide a copy of all paycheck stubs to the Reintegration facility.

I. The person is required to keep the Reintegration facility apprised of his current job title and rate of pay.

J. The person must inform the employer of his situation and past criminal history, prior to employment with the company. This is true even if the company don't care or don't ask.

K. The employer will be required to regularly update the Reintegration facility on the person and any issues that may arise.

Pre-Release: Reintegration

    Based on these rules certain employers do not hire people from the Reintegration facility. This is unfortunate for many good paying jobs only a mile, or less, from the reintegration facility are unavailable. For instance, I met with an employer three blocks from the facility and was told they would hire me but because of the Reintegration facility and its rules they would not. The job was $19.00 an hour starting with great upward potential. I instead had to settle for $13.00 an hour with no growth potential.

    I further was unable to use my skills, education and training to get a job for those jobs were not allowed. As I learned janitorial in the facility I had two janitorial job offers. The first was cleaning a dialysis center at night after it closed, it was denied because there would be no supervisor. The second was cleaning cell phone stores at night after they closed. This was denied because of the type of store and because no supervisor would be present.

    Working within the rules of Reintegration is hard. I grew up always offering for overtime to have something to do and to have extra money. However, I cannot do that in Reintegration. Some of the rules are hard to understand, but it is their world and we only live in it or get returned to Secure Confinement.

Return from Reintegration

Chapter 1: Introduction

My time in reintegration was a time filled with a plethora of loss and bad behavior on my part. I was more focused on fighting the system rather than showing the change I had made. This led to me having a few problems which in the end culminated in my return from reintegration.

The summary of notifications I received while at Reintegration can be summed up as follows: (1) Television issues (4 total); (2) Computer issues (11 Total); (3) Social behavior (2 Total); (3) Outing issues (2 Issues); (4) Work issues (3 Total); (5) Travel issues (3 Total); and (6) Other (11 Total).

The biggest issue was use of the computer and internet. At times there were children on the screen. Either I did not see them on the screen or they were unavoidable. I requested permission to click the button that turns off all pictures and was denied.

As I was denied the ability to turn the pictures off I went into an all or nothing mode and used the internet. If they wrote me up for a kid being on the screen I just used blaming or excuse making to justify it. It was their fault they did not let me turn off the pictures.

Pre-Release: Reintegration

Looking at this I can see this as the wrong response to the situation. Rather than close out the support I had (director, therapist) I need to embrace their help and work with them to create a solution to the issue that all sides can work with. I must remember that it is not my world and I cannot and do not have the authority to control, manipulate or make it work how I want it to.

The television issues were a surprise for me. At Larned prior to going to Reintegration there was no requirement that a child could be on the television screen. In fact I even owned, with permission movies, such as *Gridiron Gang, The Junction Boys, Free Willy, Free Willy 2, Free Willy 3, and Lean on Me*. Based on this I struggled to see the validity of the rule and follow it. This was my own choice and I would justify it.

Today I have a much greater appreciation for the reason of the rule and requirement. To remedy this I have continued to practice the art of not having children on my television. In fact at times individuals in the program ridicule me for it and I just ignore them. I want to change, show that I changed, go back to Reintegration and succeed.

As to social behavior I received a couple notifications for how I spoke with staff. In one instance it was perceived by me to be an issue of perception for the staff asked a question and I answered. The staff felt it was a rude answer. I did review the matter and admitted that it could have been taken as rude and I would correct the issue.

The other incident was a part of my anger cycle. I had got to the point that I did not control my anger and I lashed out being loud and argumentative with the staff member. For this I did accept my part and worked on it in anger management.

I will continue to work on social skills, though it seems to be a small part as to the reason for my return.

As to the outing issues I did not follow the rules. At the time I argued and justified my actions. I just used blaming or excuse making to justify it. Looking back at this I see that I did wrong and what steps I need to take to correct the issue.

The remaining issues are considered by me to be a repeat of the reasons that I described for the issues already. I wanted it to be my way and not their way. This then let my anger come in or obstinate and defiant behavior. At times I felt as if the roller coaster was going off the rails.

During this dark period of time a new staff member began to work in the facility. As such she did take me on many transports. During these transports there was inappropriate behavior: (1) Personal information revealed; (2) Improper route taking; and (3) Undue familiarity.

My responsibility in this situation was to inform my therapist and the director. I did not do this. This caused me to have boundary violations that continued repetitively. In fact if not curtailed or brought to light with enough force could have led me down the road to a possible offense. I do not believe I was anywhere near this point but I can see the program's responsibility in this part and lay no fault on them for returning me to Secure Confinement.

An overview of the reasons for my return has been shown. I will go into detail in the next chapter the incident with the young staff member at the facility. Keep in mind I was disciplined for the incident, but she was not.

Pre-Release: Reintegration

Chapter 2: Boundary Issue

The reason I was returned from Reintegration to Secure Confinement was for a boundary violation. This violation occurred when the staff member was transporting me to places such as work, appointments, outings, etc.

During these trips this staff member was discussing and providing me personal information about herself and her life. The rule was that because she did this I was to immediately inform my therapist and the director. I chose not to, and for this I was returned to Secure Confinement.

To assist you in understanding the full issue here I will provide the details of what she discussed and stated. Since my return I have been open and honest with the program about what she revealed or discussed and have continuously reported similar boundary violations to show that I will follow the rule.

In relaying or spelling out the information that the staff member provided I have separated it into eleven categories. Each category will specifically provide as much detail as the staff member provided to me. One must keep in mind that this occurred over a period of time, and the only reason the facility became aware was because she reported it.

Name and Age

It was custom for a staff member to provide the person in Reintegration their first name. This was not a boundary violation. What became a boundary violation is when the staff revealed her last name and then discussed her age. She stated she was eighteen and had the goal to accomplish everything early in life so she could have a relaxed middle and older age part of her life.

Family History

This staff member revealed to me that her biological father was serving time in the Hutchinson Correctional Facility. As to her childhood, she grew up in the foster care system in Kansas due to unfit or parents that were not present. She attributed the foster care system to being how she was introduced to the world of sex and a reason for her to begin having sex a lot at a very early age.

Tattoos

This staff member informed me that concerning tattoos she has three: (1) Right Wrist; (2) Left Forearm; and (3) Left Side of her Stomach. Her preference for tattoos is no color and prefers black or gray.

She stated that the tattoo on the left forearm is a remembrance for her friend that perished in a car crash at the age of ten.

Concerning the tattoo on the left side of her stomach she showed it to me. While showing me this she revealed her breasts. The breasts were covered in a bra. The tattoo looked like the playboy symbol. On the day she reported she told me this tattoo was redone and now looks like a flower. In showing me it again she revealed her breasts. The breasts were covered in a bra.

Piercings

The staff member revealed to me that she receives pleasure or enjoyment from piercings. Previously her tongue was pierced but she removed it and let it close up. She discussed the many different piercing options she was looking into.

Intimacy

Here the word intimacy is used to mean sex or the sexual part of a person. This staff member revealed much about her intimacy and issues she has.

She informed me that she began having a lot of sex at an early age. This sex was done without protection and she was fortunate to not get pregnant, for this reason she believed she could not get pregnant.

Concerning birth control she stated she is unable to have the pills for they cause migraines and condoms are more difficult as she has an allergy to latex. This causes her to avoid birth control. She stated she was going to again try birth control and hope it could work out.

While having intimacy she stated that she can only receive pleasure if vaginal intercourse is involved. Without this it usually is not a pleasurable experience.

She talked about the times she had anal sex. She tried it more than once but it was too painful so she made up her mind that certain holes are exit only.

Currently she is trying to limit herself to one sexual partner for fear of disease.

As to having intimacy with a woman she stated she tried it once. It was a friend of hers and she received pleasure while her friend was going down on her, but was displeased when it was her turn to go down on her friend for she is not into women. She stated that her friend continued to have a bisexual life but she is remaining clear of it as it does not interest her.

Children

This staff member stated that she has given birth to one child. She was sixteen at the time she got pregnant. She became pregnant because the condom broke, but based on past experience felt she would not get pregnant. This failed and at the age of seventeen she gave birth to a daughter.

In discussing the birthing process she stated it was horrible for she hemorrhaged badly and almost did not live. The dad left her to be with another sixteen year old that he knocked up and then left her also.

Relationships

As to relationships at the time, the staff revealed she was trying to be intimate with one person. She wants it to be a long term relationship but it is only a friends with benefits situation because he is just coming out of a long relationship. As to the past she stated there really was no relationship they were just sexual hookups that she participated in.

Telecommunication

The staff was allowed to have their personal cell phone with them at all times and use it if they chose to. This staff member was like much of the youth today, attached to their cell phone.

This staff member was always texting, even while she was driving. A few times it almost caused an accident. On her cell phone she had pictures of herself, her kid, and others. She would show me the pictures of herself and others, but never of her kid.

During one trip there was a deer that ran out and crashed into the vehicle. She chronicled the event by having me take photos using her cell phone. She then messaged others about it while we waited for the appropriate authorities.

She openly gave me the number to her personal cell phone. I have never used it and do not even remember it or have it written down.

It amazes me that most employers today do not allow personal cell phones at work. However, it was permissible for these staff to have and use their personal cell phone at any time.

Promiscuity

Promiscuity is when one has the character of being promiscuous. One is promiscuous when they are indiscriminate and act random or casual. This staff member was always promiscuous and free flowing with information, however, it did not stop there. She physically revealed herself and her genitalia to me on multiple occasions as if there was not a care in the world.

At one time she handed me her bag/purse and asked me to hold it. While holding it she reached in to get something at which point boxes of tampons fell out. She stated that she needed different sizes dependent upon the day. For this reason she carried a variety of sizes and types.

One time she wore some skimpy shorts and upon getting in the driver seat pulled them up and in as much as she could to reveal all of her legs and as much as she could. At another time she was wearing skimpy shorts and bent over in front of me. When she did this she pulled them up to reveal her vagina and anal area as she had no panties on.

There were times she would wear shirts that revealed her breasts with and without a bra on. She was always talking sexual and wearing very little. One time she was wearing a dress and pulled it up as far as she could. This caused her pubic region to be exposed.

This staff normally wore short dresses and would pull them up and reveal her panties and lower half. She would occasionally look over to see if I was paying attention.

Alcohol

This staff member stated she was only eighteen years old. As she was not old enough to consume alcohol legally she made it clear that she enjoyed drinking alcohol on multiple occasions. One time she revealed this to me in front of her supervisor and to my knowledge nothing occurred or happened to her.

She said her drinking habits included drinking at parties and then after work at home on almost a daily basis.

Social Life

The staff member discussed events in her personal life. I considered these to be social events or gatherings and for this reason put them here.

She stated that she enjoys going to a lot of parties and gatherings with friends. These would include skinny dipping during the day or at night.

She stated that nudity is fine and does not mind it even when around strangers. It seemed to me that she was portraying herself as a carefree spirit without a care in the world.

Pre-Release: Reintegration

Chapter 3: The Risk Posed

In order to understand the gravity of the situation in Reintegration my past offending is necessary to be understood.

I was on pre-release from a facility and was being driven everywhere by staff of the facility. One of these drivers met my attraction template and when isolated I sexually assaulted her. This is what led to my criminal offense that I did time for and made me eligible for commitment under the KSVPA. This occurred in 1994.

I went to Reintegration in 2018, twenty-six years after my offense. The Secure Commitment facility was aware of my past offending and I assumed Reintegration was also aware or should have been aware. This must not have been the case for they had me being transported in the same manner as I was in 1994, the only difference was no one was in my attraction template.

The purpose of treatment is to know the situations that led to offending, these are called high risk situations. Once recognized then the person is to draft a plan for how to avoid them. I completed all of this before Reintegration. Yet, upon placement in Reintegration they placed me in a high risk situation daily because of convenience for the facility.

What can be said for certain is that I was in this situation daily for over fourteen months and did not re-offend. Even though the staff, based on her actions, may have been willing to be intimate with me. This shows that treatment was effective and change had occurred. If treatment worked and no re-offense occurred why then return me to lock up for staff being inappropriate?

I am glad that I can celebrate the recovery I have made and the wanton and ability to control my past offending behavior. This I can say has been one of the greatest parts of treatment in Secure Confinement.

Chapter 4: Why Not Report

Since my return to Secure Confinement therapists have asked me why I did not follow the rule and report the staff member. My basic answer is simple: "Snitching is not permissible." This was a tenet that I had to learn growing up in institutions since the age of ten.

Plenty of examples of severe harm, through beatings, came to individuals who were believed or known to have snitched (told on someone). This led me to a core belief that it is not my job to police others and report their inappropriateness. The only time this was allowed is if you were in charge.

Then in addition to this core belief there are many other reasons as to why I did not report the staff member. I will go through each one of these in detail. I hope to educate many on the subject of why.

Knowledge at Reintegration

My time in Reintegration was fraught with discord. I was considered to be going against the grain more often than not by my peers and the facility. I can say this is true for I was raised to not stand for abuse or what I perceive as wrong, instead I was to stand against it. This is what I did.

For this Reintegration made it clear verbally and in writing that I am not allowed to accuse or allege staff could ever do wrong. On a day when I had an issue with staff the director got involved. After a short discussion the director point blank told me that as far as they were concerned staff could and would never do any wrong.

I received a disciplinary notice for allegedly failing to log some phone calls in my logbook. I immediately made a copy of the logbook and submitted it with the notification as evidence the calls was logged. For this the director found me guilty and stated: "...indicate that the phone numbers are now included." It is clear from my log that nothing could be added later, so in essence now the director instead of finding staff erred instead accuses me of fraudulent writing with no evidence.

The playing field is further set that I should not report staff for it will be turned on me. It is because of the verbal and written decrees that I chose to remain silent concerning the issue.

One time the air conditioner did not work in my room and it was over eighty degrees. I put in a request asking it be fixed. I was informed it was fixed, however, it was not so I put in another request. Again I received another statement it was fixed and it was not. The next request was returned to me with a statement that nothing would be done for the staff reported it was fixed.

I filed a grievance and someone came over and checked the temperature and found it was not fixed. The director was then asked why they were doing nothing. The end result for me was more strife and consequence from the director for proving staff did something wrong.

One learns by experience and my experience in Reintegration was clear: "Staff never did wrong and if I reported such it would be turned on me, as if I did the wrong." For this reason I would never tell on staff.

Treatment Goal

The goal of treatment under the KSVPA is no more victims. With this in mind if I were to have reported the incident a victim or victims would have been created. This would violate my treatment goals. The first victim would have been the person revealing the information. This is because: (1) She would have lost employment; (2) Could face criminal charges and registration requirements; and (3) She would have a hard time finding future employment.

The second victim would be her child. Her child would be a victim for: (1) She could be separated from her mom; (2) She could become a ward of the State; (3) Her mom would not be able to support her; and (4) She may be sent to a relative that is abusive. This is another victim of the incident that could occur if I reported the incident.

The last victim would be me. The law in Kansas makes it clear that if a staff member has a relationship with me it is a felony and I am a victim. K.S.A. 21-5512. This creates a third victim if were to report the incident.

I chose not to report the incident for it would be against my main treatment goal of no more victims.

Experience from Secure Confinement

In order to understand the remaining reason why I chose not to report the incident one needs to know more about me.

I was removed from my home at the age of ten and placed into the State's custody. I have been there ever since, minus a few short period where I was on pre-release from a facility. The pre-release altogether probably totaled less than one year in time frame terms.

At the end of my sentence with the Kansas Department of Corrections I received an evaluation by three different individuals prior to my commitment. These individuals held:

> "Making Recommendations for Mr. Merryfield is difficult, because he has so little base to build on. He needs structure and guidance in many areas, but will be overwhelmed by programs and counselors."

> "In my professional opinion he has not attained a level of developmental maturity or basic impulse control to get sufficient benefit from a sex offenders treatment program. I would recommend as an alternative that resources be used to obtain treatment and rehabilitation for his conduct disorder and within that program provide treatment for his sexual misconduct that would be given to an adolescent offender."

I entered Secure Confinement at the age of eighteen and as defined by the experts an immature adult with no real world experience.

I had no previous sexual experiences beyond my offending, which by the way is part of the reason I want no future victims.

Then I enter the most sexually depraved society of individuals and am subjected to this type of conversation on a daily basis, so why would I believe it is wrong. To me I am learning this is how the world operates and what people discuss.

I could not know it was wrong at the time. However, instead of taking this into consideration my treatment providers locked me up and have so far given me a prison sentence of over four years for a staff member revealing personal information to me. One may ask if this is appropriate treatment.

Pre-Release: Reintegration

Chapter 5:   The Sentence

For the staff member revealing this information and my open refusal to follow the rule and report her I was returned to Secure Confinement per a decision by the PRP.

Upon return to Secure Confinement, the therapists in Treatment Team felt it best that I start the program all over again so I was placed on tier one. I have remained there going on four years now.

Since my return to Secure Confinement the therapists continue to want to know what I received from the staff member revealing this information. The truth is that I received knowledge about a person and their sexual nature and ultimately a prison sentence, for it returned me to Secure Confinement.

I was not sexually interested in this person and did not find her attractive. I was not looking for a relationship for I knew it would violate the law and create more victims. I can honestly say that I received nothing but punishment.

As this is what I state I have received the therapists disagree with me and believe there is more than what I am telling. However, the facility administers a polygraph every six months to determine if I am telling my therapist the truth and I have passed several of them, more than eight, showing that I have told my therapist the truth. Why will they not believe me?

In order to show that I have corrected this issue I always journal and speak to my therapist when staff are creating the same boundary violations. Even though I report it staff do not get disciplined to my knowledge. It has even been done by licensed persons working in the facility (Nurses, Therapists, etc.). The one therapist decided I need to confront staff when they do create a boundary violation. I have openly complied with this requirement and then notify my therapist of its completion. Yet, I remain after three years on Tier One.

Since my return to Secure Confinement I have received more treatment and been able to complete some of my college degrees to prepare myself for the next chance I have at pre-release. I have also gained a new understanding and been open to change. I will be a better person at the next pre-release.

Chapter 6: Her Consequence

In therapy we are always asked to think of what consequence our victim had. This allows us to see the harm we cause by the offending action we took. This then reinforces our want or desire to not re-offend.

Ultimately I cannot say what this staff received if any consequence at all. After she reported the incident she kept her job and for a few days was left as the sole person to monitor me. When I left Reintegration she was still employed and working at Reintegration.

I do not believe she suffered a consequence. However, if she was terminated for this incident then my previous statement concerning the consequences she would suffer have come to fruition.

I can say for sure that if her intent was for ill-gotten means, i.e. returning me to Secure Confinement, she succeeded. I will not dwell on this and will move forward with my treatment.

Pre-Release: Reintegration

Back to Secure Confinement

Chapter 1: Introduction

One gets to Reintegration by completing the treatment program in Secure Confinement. This means they have acquired the necessary skills and demonstrated an ability to use them effectively. Does this mean the person is never returned to Secure Confinement? The answer is no.

If the person does something the Reintegration facility does not like the Reintegration facility can and will send the individual back to Secure Confinement. The PRP makes the final decision as to whether or not the individual should be returned to Secure Confinement. Just how does this process work and is it therapeutic?

Chapter 2: Therapy vs. Discipline

For purposes of this chapter we must first state what treatment is and what discipline is.

Treatment is something meant to be beneficial to the person to help them correct what is deemed as an inappropriate or unacceptable behavior.

Discipline is basically punishment, something meant to be uncomfortable to the person to the point it ensures they do not do the same behavior in the future.

In order to make it to Reintegration the person has to make significant change in his condition and complete a certain amount of treatment. What if he has a problem in Reintegration and needs to return to Secure Confinement? Will he be punished or will it be a therapeutic move? What if the Resident feels there is an issue and requests a return to secure confinement?

Until recently it could be argued that the move was therapeutic and the individual would remain only long enough to correct the issue for which he returned. The administration and therapists of 2021 and 2022 have taken measures to ensure it is punitive, even if the Resident asks to go back and work on an issue. For a proper review we must look to the statutes and the internal policies and procedures of KDADS.

The statute (K.S.A. 59-29a02) holds that the PRP is a group of individuals appointed by the secretary for aging and disability services to evaluate a person's progress in the sexually violent predator treatment program. KDADS internally defines the PRP as a group of persons familiar with the typical behavior patterns of sexual offenders and who understand the challenges faced by these individuals as they attempt to negotiate their re-entry into society, a society which may be hostile to their return.

It now appears that by having the PRP decide, whether to return one to Secure Confinement, makes it a treatment decision. The author agrees wholeheartedly with this, but it is what occurs after the decision to return is made that makes it discipline.

Once the person is returned to Secure Confinement the PRP no longer has any say over his care and treatment. In fact the policies of KDADS dictate that the following will occur: (1) The Resident will be issued a Disciplinary Notification form and be subjected to the Disciplinary Process of Secure Confinement; (2) Treatment Team at Secure Confinement will place the individual on Tier One (the lowest); and (3) The person will be reduced to Blue on the privilege level system. Before we discuss each of the three in detail we must first keep in mind that policy dictates only the PRP has the authority to raise a Tier level, if this is true why then do they not dictate what tier the person returns on?

The disciplinary system within the Secure Confinement is meant for one thing: punishment. So if a person has an issue he needs additional therapy for, even if he voluntarily returns he is subjected to discipline.

The consequences can include: (1) Restriction Status; (2) Loss of property; (3) Loss of chance to regain freedom; and (4) A bad report to the committing court; to name a few. Some of these are liberty interests protected by the United States Constitution. Merely subjecting the person to this system for every return automatically means that it is not a therapeutic move rather it is a disciplinary procedure.

The second part is that Treatment Team at Secure Confinement determines where the person is placed (Tier 1,

2, or 3). In most all cases the person is placed on Tier 1 and has to start the program over. This creates a problem for the Treatment Team is not part of the Reintegration facility and does not know the exact facts of what occurred or what the person's experience was there. They are making a decision in the blind.

As the majority of the time Treatment Team starts a person over at tier one for returning this can only be said to be punitive and not treatment based. In addition then Treatment Team issues a disciplinary notification themselves as required by the internal policies. It is clearly a disciplinary measure rather than a therapeutic decision.

The final item to review is the privilege level system. This system is not applicable in Reintegration. Prior to going to Reintegration the person would normally have been on the highest level (Purple). At Reintegration the freedom is greater than this so coming back and being put on Blue automatically, two steps below purple, seems egregious and overbearing. In addition it is the lowest which means the person is not eligible for a job, and has very little property or privileges. If the move is for therapeutic reasons, then why is a severe consequence and loss issued to the person? The answer is that the move is punitive rather than therapeutic.

In a therapeutic return one would expect to be put on the level that would ensure that he receives treatment for that which returned him.

In this author's case the issue was during transport to and from outings. This he will not experience unless he is on tier two, however, they placed him on tier one. As such how should he work on the issue that caused his return? He cannot therefore the proper therapeutic cause would have been to return him on tier two, as he was not it can only be said to be punitive.

The statements and actions of the current therapists and administration make it clear that they are going to make it the most degrading and punitive measure they can if one returns from Reintegration. This means they are intending to prevent or deter one from coming back, even if they feel they might be a risk because something is not working out. The law defines this as punishment.

In addition it raises the concern that the taxpayers are at risk because a resident certainly does not want to come back to the worst position possible and start all over so rather than request and go back to the help they choose to stay. This only creates a bigger risk for the community.

In addition returning one, who violated a rule, did not lapse, relapse or put the public at risk, and making them start over as if they had learned or did no treatment previously is wrong. This alienates the person from treatment and causes them to hamper the process and possibly harm others by making it non-therapeutic for them.

It appears the goal is to be punitive upon a return from Reintegration rather than rehabilitative or therapeutically aligned. Each person will have to make their own decision and go from there. In doing so keep in mind that those in the secure confinement facility were not in or a part of the Reintegration Facility and their decision on where to place the Resident is made with no firsthand knowledge of what, if any specific treatment they need.

Chapter 3: Media

As discussed previously I received a notification or write up concerning music or had music restricted from me. For a quick recap the list is as follows:

Little Toy Guns-Carrie Underwood

When I'm Gone-Eminem

Blown Away-Carrie Underwood

Ms. Jackson-Outcast

Hell is for Children-Pat Benatar

Down With the Sickness-Disturbed

Mother-Danzig

Jesus Take the Wheel-Carrie Underwood

Alyssa Lies-Jason Michael Carol

Mockingbird-Eminem

Temporary Home-Carrie Underwood

I Wanna Love You-Akon

It is true that before going to Reintegration a licensed therapist approved this music and at Reintegration a director with no background in the field of therapy deemed them to be un-therapeutic. What has happened since my return to Secure Confinement?

Pre-Release: Reintegration

Upon being returned to Secure Confinement I requested permission to receive certain music CD's in the mail. After a lengthy (6 months or more) review by a licensed therapist the music was deemed appropriate and I was and am allowed to have it. This includes:

Little Toy Guns-Carrie Underwood

Blown Away-Carrie Underwood

Jesus Take the Wheel-Carrie Underwood

Temporary Home-Carrie Underwood

Alyssa Lies-Jason Michael Carol

This appears to show an even further an abuse of power by a director in Reintegration. Further, as was shown earlier within this book Reintegration is just an internal move within Secure Confinement, so why are the rules different at each place? I cannot render a decision other than to say it is nothing more than a game whereby the confined person suffers abuse.

Pre-Release: Reintegration

Past, Present, and Future Verbal Boundary Violations

Chapter 1: Introduction

In this book it has been shown that the author was returned from Reintegration to secure Confinement for a staff member revealing too much information about herself to him verbally. In order to put this into perspective the author is going to illustrate how this is a daily occurrence at all parts of confinement under the KSVPA.

To make a proper illustration the author will present this in three different sections: (1) Prior to Reintegration; (2) During Reintegration; and (3) At Secure Confinement, after his return. The one thing to be noted is that most if not all of the incidents have been reported and no discipline has occurred to any staff member, to the knowledge the author has.

One will have many questions after review of this section and the author is probably unable to answer most of those questions. It will be noticed that there is a rampant boundary violation that occurs frequently.

Chapter 2: Prior to Reintegration

I was in the Secure Confinement portion under the KSVPA for eighteen years before going to Reintegration. During these years there were verbal boundary violations, but I did not recognize them as such for it was a normal occurrence.

There was a time in Secure Confinement where a staff member was leaning over a counter. As she did this she began explaining that this was her preferred sexual position. She enjoyed men taking her from behind in this position both vaginally and anally. She discussed some of her experiences from that position in detail.

In Secure Confinement a staff was having a conversation with me and she turned it into a sexual conversation. She talked about how many kids she has and that when she gets pregnant one cannot tell as she does not get a belly. She then discussed that she preferred a man to take her from behind, but that anal sex was not allowed.

In Secure Confinement a female staff member began discussing herself and her sexual preferences. She stated that she had a flower tattoo on her pubic region. She stated that she loved sex a lot and would have sex with men to get pregnant to make money off of them.

I was playing cards with a female staff member one day and she began discussing her sex life. She stated that she had to be fixed for she was always getting pregnant, so much so that she received the nickname "Fertile Myrtle." She discussed that she had four kids, all girls.

One day a staff member was discussing that she tried a new cake recipe at home. The name of the cake recipe was "Better than Sex Cake." She explained to me in great detail that she did not know if it was better than sex for she had never had a sexual experience before. She discussed that she felt it was better to wait.

During therapy a therapist was discussing her personal sex life. In doing so she was detailing different positions and whether they provided pleasure. She would discuss her experience with pregnancy and other life issues.

Staff were always discussing their personal lives and sexual preferences with persons in the facility. It was quite rampant.

Chapter 3: During Reintegration

While being transported at Reintegration to places staff would discuss themselves and their personal lives. During these trips there were other incidents where staff would reveal information.

During a trip a staff member began discussing her teenage years. More specifically, that her sister was a teen mother and due to the severe complications of it, she did not have sex until she was married. She discussed this in detail. At times she would show pictures of her husband and at the store if she ran into her husband would make sure we met him. At times she would show security footage of her home on her telephone.

The staff member that reported herself, the one I was returned from Reintegration for, was an open book, as discussed earlier. There is very little about her that is unknown to me.

While in the community (outings, work, appointments, etc.) most of the conversations I heard were of a sexual nature. At work I would have some discussing their personal sex lives and what they liked and disliked. It was not uncommon.

Pre-Release: Reintegration

Pre-Release: Reintegration

Chapter 4: At Secure Confinement, the Second Time

After being returned for the boundary violation I believed that the program had changed and it would not occur again. However, this was not the case and for that reason I will discuss recent events in which the boundary violation has occurred again.

While on the living unit the staff was discussing issues of their personal life and that of other staff. Specifically there was talk of incidents of domestic violence, family and kids.

I was sitting in the day hall and a female staff member sat down and began discussing her pregnancy and her kids. She was discussing her sex life and that she could not get enough sex.

While I was in the day hall staff was discussing their personal romances, domestic violence they suffered, and current situations of domestic violence occurring in their community.

An administrative official of the program informed me that staff do not have to follow the rules of the facility if it is inconvenient for them.

Pre-Release: Reintegration

While doing my job in the facility, the direct supervisor discussed her personal life. She stated that in high school she was a member of band and males and females changed in the same room. During a trip some were caught having sex on the bus. She then discussed in detail the time she walked in on her boyfriend having sex with a fourteen year old girl. Then she gave details about other staff and their personal lives. This staff carried on a sexual relation with a resident in the office.

A staff member was discussing her pregnancy and due date and her doctor appointments about the pregnancy. I was at work and could not leave the area, however, the supervisor did comment that the staff was being inappropriate.

I was standing at the door to my room (cell) while a Unit Leader (Licensed Administrative Official) and one staff searched my room. These two were holding a conversation, loud enough for me to hear, about their kids, the babysitter they use, and the school for their kids.

I attended a class led by a licensed therapist. The licensed therapist began discussing her personal life, specifically: (1) Her age; (2) Her sexual orientation (openly gay); (3) She was addicted to drugs and alcohol since the age of eighteen; and (4) She is still recovering from drug addiction and is in treatment. I met with the licensed therapist that led the class and explained to her that the information she provided was inappropriate.

I met with my therapist and the lead/head therapist for the program. Both informed me that I need to do more than just report the inappropriateness of staff. They want me to confront the staff. There are many dangers inherent in this, both from staff and my peers and when I vocalized this they had an indifferent attitude.

I was in a class and the instructor deviated from the material and began discussing her personal life. After class I put it in my journal and then provided a copy to my therapist. On April 14, 2021, I spoke with this instructor, with my therapist present, and informed her of the inappropriate discussion. At the next class with this instructor a resident asked her personal questions, following from the week before, and with an indignant and condescending attitude the instructor stated: "Well I guess I am not supposed to discuss that anymore."

Pre-Release: Reintegration

I was attending a class and the instructor began discussing her children. After class I put in a journal entry concerning this incident and after providing a copy to my therapist requested a meeting with my therapist and this instructor to discuss the issue. At one point I was able to discuss it with her supervisor and was informed by the supervisor that staff work multiple hours and therefore will make a mistake or have boundary violations and it is excusable.

I went to yard for some fresh air. At the yard a staff member had paperwork spread out on the table in plain sight of all at the yard. The paperwork revealed: (1) Her home address; (2) Her birth date; (3) Her telephone number; and (4) Her e-mail address.

As I sat in the day hall typing on the computer two staff were having conversations with residents. They were discussing what days they were going to be working and which days they were not, and one was going to go home and drink and do drugs.

I attended a therapy class led by a female therapist. In this class the subject was intimate relationships (dating). The conversation skewed off into a discussion of sex. The therapist and others were discussing that the size of the man's penis does not matter when it comes to sex. Per the therapist if the man feels the woman is loose there is something the woman can do to resolve the issue. It takes communication. In fact she stated that she had enough control to ensure that no matter what size the man was he would always feel it was tight with her.

A staff member saw the story about the shortage of baby formula. This prompted her to discuss that she had kids and when she did she always breast fed her children. Her opinion was that if more women did this the issue would not occur.

A nurse was working the unit and discussed her recent experience with having a child. She was very clear that she enjoys sex but could not stand to have another child. She discussed how her life had changed based on giving birth.

Pre-Release: Reintegration

Past, Present and Future Visual Boundary Violations

Chapter 1: Introduction

In this book it has been shown that the author was returned from Reintegration to secure Confinement for a staff member revealing too much information about herself to him verbally.

In order to more fully put this into perspective the author is going to illustrate how physical boundary violations, through visual means, occurs on a rampant basis within the program under the KSVPA.

In treatment the author learned that the way a person dresses does not mean they want anything. The author fully agrees with this and believes that in society one is free to dress how they want, but should this be true in a facility wherein there are men that are there for lack of control and have been denied sex for many years?

The question has been answered in both positive and negative fashion. I will say that for a secure facility it is interesting that staff is not in uniform or that the facility exerts no dress code of any kind.

Concerning staff and what they wear, act or do, I will describe this in three sections: Before Reintegration; At

Reintegration; and Once Returned to Secure Confinement. As I was not always keeping track of this I do not have specific dates in some sections.

One will have many questions after review of this section and the author is probably unable to answer most of those questions. It will be noticed that there is a rampant boundary violation that occurs frequently.

Chapter 2:   Prior to Reintegration

As I sat in the day hall one day a female staff member sat there with low cut pants on. Based on how she was sitting the pants revealed her entire butt. Once she was made aware of it she did nothing to correct it. Then she was engaging in a conversation with persons confined about her anal sex experiences. She made clear that she preferred a man to anally penetrate her.

I was in the day hall one day and a female staff member was sitting there having a conversation about her sex life and how many kids she had. She was wearing tights that revealed her entire bottom half.

At work a female supervisor informed me that she went to a correctional facility to visit her boyfriend. While there the male guards strip searched her. Her complaint was that they did not pay her for the strip search. She made it clear that she would reveal her body for a certain sum of money to anyone. She normally wore see through shirts and other clothing.

I was called to an office by an administrative official. What I thought was a purposeful meeting was not instead the female was trying to groom me. She lowered her shirt and showed me her shoulders in a sensuous way while asking questions. I notice she had a tattoo between her shoulder blades it was a circle in color with jagged edges around it. I made an excuse and left. This official has been investigated for sex with another resident but never removed or disciplined to my knowledge.

Chapter 3: During Reintegration

The most promiscuous one is the one that provided me the information that caused my return from Reintegration. She came to work wearing barely anything. She would have short dresses on, skimpy shorts, see through shirts, and tight shirts. This led to her revealing her uncovered breasts and vagina on more than one occasion during transports. She also openly lifted her clothes to reveal her tattoos to me, revealing more of her sexual organs.

On certain transports, when she was wearing thin skimpy shorts, she would pull them up as far as she could thereby revealing as much as she could. One time she had on extremely tight shorts and nothing underneath, she acted as if she dropped something and bent over in front of me revealing all.

Chapter 4: At Secure Confinement, the Second Time

There was a dark skinned female staff member working the unit. She was wearing a white see through shirt and her entire chest was visible. When she went by me it was noticed that she was sagging her sweatpants so low that you could see her entire rear, at that point it was noticed that it was not a white shirt, rather it was a singlet.

An administrator for the facility came on the unit wearing a tight shirt. It allowed for her nipples to be seen in plain view. She was on the unit for about fifteen minutes.

A nurse was working the unit and had a sleeveless shirt on. This revealed her breasts, including side boob, and the bra she was wearing.

A staff member working the unit was wearing a set of pastel colored scrubs. The color was so light that it was see through. One could see the parts of her butt cheek that were not covered by her panties and one could see the entire set of panties she was wearing.

One time a therapist was taking me to class. The female therapist was wearing a low cut top. She dropped something and when she bent over to pick it up she turned towards me first causing all of her breasts to be seen due to the low cut top.

One day a therapist picked me up for class. She was wearing a white see through shirt. During the entire class she revealed her entire breasts.

A nurse was working the unit and wore a white see through shirt and tights for pants. This caused her entire body to be revealed.

A dark skinned female staff member wore see through white pants and shirt. This revealed all her genitalia which was covered by bra and panties. At one point she stopped and bent over to tie her shoe, revealing her entire bottom.

Double Standard Concerning
Boundary Violation

Pre-Release: Reintegration

Chapter 1: The Incident

As this book shows the author was returned for staff relaying personal information to him and then he chose not to report it. I will admit this is a boundary violation, but can it be said to be equally applied? To that, I answer there is a double standard.

At one point in Secure Confinement an individual began a relationship with staff. This relationship included the passing of information and a sexual relationship. The staff member quit working at the facility but maintained the relationship with the individual.

The staff of Secure Confinement were aware of the relationship but did not consequent the staff member or the resident. In fact they did not even pursue criminal charges under K.S.A. 21-5512, as was their duty.

The individual eventually made it to Reintegration. The relationship with the ex-staff member continued to the point they were married. Reintegration was fine with this relationship and allowed it to occur. They even allowed them to meet, move in together, and have a life together. After he was released from Conditional Release they now have children together.

You may ask what the difference between this and my situation. I cannot answer to you why Secure Confinement and Reintegration allow certain relationships and deny others. What I can tell you is that there was no relationship between the staff and me and I was not seeking one. There was no inappropriateness on my part and I did not force her to do what she did. I can tell you that I have suffered greatly for it though.

There is an administrator that was investigated for having sex with one confined in the program. The individual confined admitted it was true. Yet, rather than charge this person as the laws in Kansas dictate, and as she has done to other staff, she has been allowed to continue to work in the program.

This is just some examples of the double standard used by those that are in charge of Secure Confinement and Reintegration.

Pre-Release: Reintegration

Potential Victim

Chapter 1: Introduction

When you first think potential victim you may think of a person that the sex offender likes and would offend against, in therapy terms one in their attraction template. This would be a common understanding, however, in Reintegration under the KSVPA this term takes on a whole new meaning.

This is an important subject for in the section where I discuss all my write-ups they constantly used the term PV. Was I truly seeing one that was a PV for me or is it just a broad term they use so they can write everyone up.

In Secure Confinement one is required to complete a full RPP with an attraction template included before moving to Reintegration. I did this, however, when I moved to Reintegration they discarded my RPP (About 45 Pages) and handed me a four to six page one they created.

I will use this section of the book to discuss who or how Reintegration views and uses the term PV.

Chapter 2: Television

When it comes to television the rules are simple: if the person on the screen is under the age of eighteen, or appears to be, you are in the wrong. This is even true for one who has offended against adults only, there is no differentiation.

In Secure Confinement this is not true and I even had movies approved by therapists, such as: (1) *Free Willy*; (2) *Major Payne*; and (3) *The Goonies*, etc. In Secure Confinement there was no staff being a TV monitor and disciplining you because of a child on the TV screen. This caused me to struggle in this area in Reintegration.

The best avenue for one is to never watch television and instead only watch the movies they approve or play the video games they approve. This is the only way to ensure not to be disciplined, even if a child is not on the screen.

I would also question that if a child on the television screen creates a risk that the person will offend again, what are they doing in Reintegration?

Chapter 3: Internet

When it comes to internet the rules are simple: if a picture of a person under the age of eighteen comes on, you are in the wrong. You also are not allowed to turn on a pop-up blocker, or use analog internet as discussed previously to prevent the images from showing up.

In Secure Confinement there is no internet and they do not tech the usage of the internet or computers for the IT Department does not let them or because they choose not to.

While I was in Reintegration my RPP stated I was not to be looking at children. The way internet is monitored is they record what is on the screen and days, weeks or months later look at the recording. If they see a person under eighteen was on the screen they write you up and state you were looking at children. There are two problems here: (1) This is an assumption; and (2) Polygraphs disprove it as false.

One assumes just because the child is on the screen that you are looking at it. If this is true why is the same not true when you are in the community and a child is within eyesight? The great saying that assuming makes an ass out of you and me, can be no more true than in this situation, which is then proven by polygraph testing.

In Reintegration one must submit to a polygraph once every six months. During my time I took several and passed them all. What is most notable is that they always asked if I was viewing children on the internet and I said no. The test proved I was not lying. So why continue to write me up just because it is on the screen and you deny me the ability to prevent it from showing? It can be said to be punitive.

I would also question that if a child on the internet screen creates a risk that the person will offend again, what are they doing in Reintegration?

Chapter 4: In the Community

As the person is in Reintegration they are out and about in the community on a daily basis. This could be for work, for an outing, a leisure activity, or medical appointment. During these trips one will see or be around children, does this mean he will be written up for it and disciplined, as he would if they appeared on the TV or on the internet screen? The answer is no.

Why there is a difference between seeing children in real life and on the TV or internet is something I could never figure out or grasp while I was in Reintegration. I raised the issue with the director on several occasions and even the therapist and received no answer.

It is true in Reintegration that one is supposed to go to places at times less likely to have these minors around. This is a tool they do allow for you to use, unless it becomes inconvenient for staff. During most of my trips to the community it would be to places that didn't allow minors (Casinos, etc.) or at times that they were likely not to be there (Wal-Mart, 0200 AM).

Pre-Release: Reintegration

If I had indirect or possible direct contact I had to log it in my logbook and report it. To be clear direct contact was an instant trip back to Secure Confinement unless it was not your fault. For instance, once I was at a store with staff and we saw a couple coming by as we were ready to exit an aisle. We waited and figured there was no child, as we went out the aisle the child appeared. The child was fifteen feet behind the parents and being quiet. This was unavoidable contact.

The rules are more relaxed when one is in the community, whereas concerning television or internet it is a strict no policy and you are not allowed to use certain tools to prevent it.

Chapter 5: The Purpose of Treatment

A person committed under the KSVPA begins the treatment process at Secure Confinement. The structure of the treatment is to assist the individual in recognizing why or how he offended previously. Once this information is gathered then the individual begins the process of changing the behaviors so he does not offend in the same manner.

Not only does the statutes of the KSVPA, but the treatment policy under the KSVPA as well, dictate that the person is not to be released to Reintegration, Transition, or Conditional Release unless they are safe. It does not mean cured, it just means that the likelihood of offending is reduced to a statistically safe probability.

Based on the purpose and intent of treatment, why is seeing a child on the TV or Internet a danger for the person and/or to society? Are they trying to admit they did not treat the issue that causes the person to offend? Why is it the same for one that only has adult victims?

Before we go in depth into these questions we must first remember the history of the KSVPA. In 1994 the Legislature enacted the KSVPA due to the actions of serial rapist Charles Gideon. This person offended adults and therefore the intent was not necessarily aimed at protecting children. It became a part of the KSVPA to protect children with the first commitment under the KSVPA, Leroy Hendricks.

In essence the Reintegration house is so focused on protecting children that adult victims might even be victimized before the Reintegration facility knows it. This is a misplaced focus and they should instead be willing to accept that their treatment was effective. At that point then if the TV or Internet was causing one to become a greater risk than they would know and deal with it.

However, Reintegration just wants to block everything out. Is this helpful or harmful? We must remember that after Reintegration the person is living in society on his own without Reintegration breathing down his neck. This means that he will have internet and TV and not be forced to not see kids. Does this mean they have swept the monster under the rug and instead release one with this problem? The answer would be yes. This should not occur and as a society we should hold them accountable.

Since Secure Confinement does not monitor TV and provides no internet, that is the first failure of the State. Then Reintegration uses forced abstinence treatment methods and denies use of appropriate tools. This then denies the person the ability to learn how to use these items with the appropriate tools in place. This is the second failure of the State. Do we just continue to allow this to occur?

As a society that is not informed we would allow it to continue. However, after you have read this book you are informed and it is upon you to make your voice heard on the matter.

E-Mail in Reintegration

Pre-Release: Reintegration

Chapter 1: The Consequence of E-Mail

Electronic Mail (E-Mail) is a daily part of life in society today that comes with the internet. In Reintegration they do allow for one to have an E-Mail address but under specific rules.

When I went to Reintegration I had two personal E-Mail accounts. As I had these they informed me that I could not use them and would have to delete them. I complained and in the end I was allowed to keep them but not use them. In accords with the Kansas Offender Registration Act (KORA), I had to list both E-Mail addresses when I registered.

The Reintegration facility assigned me an E-Mail account, but this was harmful. The rules of Reintegration is that you can only use it for job purposes or account maintenance as most online accounts require an E-Mail address. For this reason many of my accounts had the E-Mail address they provided me linked to it. This is what caused the problem.

Once you leave Reintegration they keep the E-Mail address and do all they can to block you out of it. Because of this I still have accounts today that I cannot access because I no longer have access to the E-Mail address they provided me. This has caused me to lose accounts and money.

For me this is a lesson that I will never forget. When I return to Reintegration I will link none of my accounts using the E-Mail they provide. Instead I will have to link them to my E-Mail addresses and have family manage them for me.

Kansas Offender Registration Act

Chapter 1:   Introduction

In Kansas certain individuals that have been found guilty of a crime are required to comply with the Kansas Offender Registration Act (KORA). In 2001 the Kansas Legislature amended the KORA to require lifetime registration for one deemed to be a Sexually Violent Predator on or after July 1, 2001.

The KORA sets very strict duties upon any facility that releases one who is required to register and on the person that is required to register. The consequence for the person is a new felony on their record and a new prison sentence.

How does the KORA play a part concerning Reintegration? It plays a huge part and will be discussed in as much detail as necessary herein.

Chapter 2: The KORA

The Kansas Legislature enacted the KORA in 1993. The intent and purpose was to provide a database and place where one could look and see if their neighbor or someone in the area was a dangerous offender.

The provisions of the KORA are located in the Criminal Code section of the Kansas Statutes Annotated, specifically K.S.A. 22-4901 et seq.

One who is subject to registration under the KORA is required to report quarterly to the Sheriff and update their registration. In addition they are required to register within three days of moving to a new address, gaining new employment, becoming a student, or one of the many other reasons listed in the KORA.

In order to know what months the individual is required to register in, they base it on the month of their birthday. To make this easier use the following chart:

January	February	March
April	May	June
July	August	September
October	November	December

Pre-Release: Reintegration

To use the chart find the month of your birthday, then go up and down (column) and those are the months you are required to register in.

Now let's take a look at the entire Act. For this we are enclosing it herein updated and complete through the 2023 Kansas Legislative Session.

K.S.A. 22-4901   **Citation of Act**

K.S.A. 22-4901 through 22-4911 and 22-4913, and amendments thereto, shall be known and may be cited as the Kansas offender registration act.

K.S.A. 22-4902   **Definitions**

As used in the Kansas offender registration act, unless the context otherwise requires:

(a)   "Offender" means:

    (1)   A sex offender;

    (2)   A violent offender;

    (3)   A drug offender;

(4) Any person who has been required to register under out-of-state law or is otherwise required to be registered; and

(5) Any person required by court order to register for an offense not otherwise required as provided in the Kansas offender registration act.

(b) "Sex offender" includes any person who:

(1) On or after April 14, 1994, is convicted of any sexually violent crime;

(2) On or after July 1, 2002, is adjudicated as a juvenile offender for an act which, if committed by an adult, would constitute the commission of a sexually violent crime, unless the court, on the record, finds that the act involved non-forcible sexual conduct, the victim was at least 14 years of age and the offender was not more than four years older than the victim;

(3) Has been determined to be a sexually violent predator;

(4) On or after July 1, 1997, is convicted of any of the following crimes when one of the parties involved is less than 18 years of age:

    (A) Adultery, as defined in K.S.A. 21-3507, prior to its repeal, or K.S.A. 2022 Supp. 21-5511, and amendments thereto;

    (B) Criminal sodomy, as defined in K.S.A. 21-3505(a)(1), prior to its repeal, or K.S.A. 2022 Supp. 21-5504(a)(1) or (a)(2), and amendments thereto;

    (C) Promoting prostitution, as defined in K.S.A. 21-3513, prior to its repeal, or K.S.A. 2022 Supp. 21-6420, prior to its amendment by section 17 of chapter 120 of the 2013 Session Laws of Kansas on July 1, 2013;

    (D) Patronizing a prostitute, as defined in K.S.A. 21-3515, prior to its repeal, or K.S.A. 2022 Supp. 21-6421, prior to its amendment by section 18 of chapter

120 of the 2013 Session Laws of Kansas on July 1, 2013; or

(E) Lewd and lascivious behavior, as defined in K.S.A. 21-3508, prior to its repeal, or K.S.A. 2022 Supp. 21-5513, and amendments thereto;

(5) Is convicted of sexual battery, as defined in K.S.A. 21-3517, prior to its repeal, or K.S.A. 2022 Supp. 21-5505(a), and amendments thereto;

(6) Is convicted of sexual extortion, as defined in K.S.A. 2022 Supp. 21-5515, and amendments thereto;

(7) Is convicted of breach of privacy, as defined in K.S.A. 2022 Supp. 21-6101(a)(6), (a)(7) or (a)(8), and amendments thereto;

(8) Is convicted of an attempt, conspiracy or criminal solicitation, as defined in K.S.A. 21-3301, 21-3302 or 21-3303, prior to their repeal, or K.S.A. 2022 Supp. 21-5301, 21-

5302, 21-5303, and amendments thereto, of an offense defined in this subsection; or

(9) Has been convicted of an offense that is comparable to any crime defined in this subsection, or any out-of-state conviction for an offense that under the laws of this state would be an offense defined in this subsection.

(c) "Sexually violent crime" means:

(1) Rape, as defined in K.S.A. 21-3502, prior to its repeal, or K.S.A. 2022 Supp. 21-5503, and amendments thereto;

(2) Indecent liberties with a child, as defined in K.S.A. 21-3503, prior to its repeal, or K.S.A. 2022 Supp. 21-5506(a), and amendments thereto;

(3) Aggravated indecent liberties with a child, as defined in K.S.A. 21-3504, prior to its repeal, or K.S.A. 2022 Supp. 21-5506(b), and amendments thereto;

(4) Criminal sodomy, as defined in K.S.A. 21-3505(a)(2) or (a)(3), prior to its repeal, or K.S.A.

2022 Supp. 21-5504(a)(3) or (a)(4), and amendments thereto;

(5) Aggravated criminal sodomy, as defined in K.S.A. 21-3506, prior to its repeal, or K.S.A. 2022 Supp. 21-5504(b), and amendments thereto;

(6) Indecent solicitation of a child, as defined in K.S.A. 21-3510, prior to its repeal, or K.S.A. 2022 Supp. 21-5508(a), and amendments thereto;

(7) Aggravated indecent solicitation of a child, as defined in K.S.A. 21-3511, prior to its repeal, or K.S.A. 2022 Supp. 21-5508(b), and amendments thereto;

(8) Sexual exploitation of a child, as defined in K.S.A. 21-3516, prior to its repeal, or K.S.A. 2022 Supp. 21-5510, and amendments thereto;

(9) Aggravated sexual battery, as defined in K.S.A. 21-3518, prior to its repeal, or K.S.A. 2022 Supp. 21-5505(b), and amendments thereto;

(10) Aggravated incest, as defined in K.S.A. 21-3603, prior to its repeal, or K.S.A. 2022 Supp. 21-5604(b), and amendments thereto;

(11) Electronic solicitation, as defined in K.S.A. 21-3523, prior to its repeal, and K.S.A. 2022 Supp. 21-5509, and amendments thereto;

(12) Unlawful sexual relations, as defined in K.S.A. 21-3520, prior to its repeal, or K.S.A. 2022 Supp. 21-5512, and amendments thereto;

(13) Aggravated human trafficking, as defined in K.S.A. 21-3447, prior to its repeal, or K.S.A. 2022 Supp. 21-5426(b), and amendments thereto, if committed in whole or in part for the purpose of the sexual gratification of the defendant or another;

(14) Commercial sexual exploitation of a child, as defined in K.S.A. 2022 Supp. 21-6422, and amendments thereto;

(15) Promoting the sale of sexual relations, as defined in K.S.A. 2022 Supp. 21-6420, and amendments thereto;

(16) Internet trading in child pornography or aggravated internet trading in child pornography, as defined in K.S.A. 2021 Supp. 21-5514, and amendments thereto;

(17) Any conviction or adjudication for an offense that is comparable to a sexually violent crime as defined in this subsection, or any out-of-state conviction or adjudication for an offense that under the laws of this state would be a sexually violent crime as defined in this subsection;

(18) An attempt, conspiracy or criminal solicitation, as defined in K.S.A. 21-3301, 21-3302 or 21-3303, prior to their repeal, or K.S.A. 2022 Supp. 21-5301, 21-5302, 21-5303, and amendments thereto, of a sexually violent crime, as defined in this subsection; or

(19) Any act that has been determined beyond a reasonable doubt to have been sexually motivated, unless the court, on the record, finds that the act involved non-forcible sexual

conduct, the victim was at least 14 years of age and the offender was not more than four years older than the victim. As used in this paragraph, "sexually motivated" means that one of the purposes for which the defendant committed the crime was for the purpose of the defendant's sexual gratification.

(d) "Sexually violent predator" means any person who, on or after July 1, 2001, is found to be a sexually violent predator pursuant to K.S.A. 59-29a01 et seq., and amendments thereto.

(e) "Violent offender" includes any person who:

(1) On or after July 1, 1997, is convicted of any of the following crimes:

(A) Capital murder, as defined in K.S.A. 21-3439, prior to its repeal, or K.S.A. 2022 Supp. 21-5401, and amendments thereto;

(B) Murder in the first degree, as defined in K.S.A. 21-3401, prior to its repeal, or

K.S.A. 2022 Supp. 21-5402, and amendments thereto;

(C) Murder in the second degree, as defined in K.S.A. 21-3402, prior to its repeal, or K.S.A. 2022 Supp. 21-5403, and amendments thereto;

(D) Voluntary manslaughter, as defined in K.S.A. 21-3403, prior to its repeal, or K.S.A. 2022 Supp. 21-5404, and amendments thereto;

(E) Involuntary manslaughter, as defined in K.S.A. 21-3404, prior to its repeal, or K.S.A. 2022 Supp. 21-5405(a)(1), (a)(2) or (a)(4), and amendments thereto. The provisions of this paragraph shall not apply to violations of K.S.A. 2021 Supp. 21-5405(a)(3), and amendments thereto, that occurred on or after July 1, 2011, through July 1, 2013;

(F) Kidnapping, as defined in K.S.A. 21-3420, prior to its repeal, or K.S.A. 2022

Supp. 21-5408(a), and amendments thereto;

(G) Aggravated kidnapping, as defined in K.S.A. 21-3421, prior to its repeal, or K.S.A. 2022 Supp. 21-5408(b), and amendments thereto;

(H) Criminal restraint, as defined in K.S.A. 21-3424, prior to its repeal, or K.S.A. 2022 Supp. 21-5411, and amendments thereto, except by a parent, and only when the victim is less than 18 years of age; or

(I) Aggravated human trafficking, as defined in K.S.A. 21-3447, prior to its repeal, or K.S.A. 2022 Supp. 21-5426(b), and amendments thereto, if not committed in whole or in part for the purpose of the sexual gratification of the defendant or another;

(2) On or after July 1, 2006, is convicted of any person felony and the court makes a finding on

the record that a deadly weapon was used in the commission of such person felony;

(3) Has been convicted of an offense that is comparable to any crime defined in this subsection, any out-of-state conviction for an offense that under the laws of this state would be an offense defined in this subsection; or

(4) Is convicted of an attempt, conspiracy or criminal solicitation, as defined in K.S.A. 21-3301, 21-3302 or 21-3303, prior to their repeal, or K.S.A. 2022 Supp. 21-5301, 21-5302 and 21-5303, and amendments thereto, of an offense defined in this subsection.

(f) "Drug offender" includes any person who, on or after July 1, 2007:

(1) Is convicted of any of the following crimes:

(A) Unlawful manufacture or attempting such of any controlled substance or controlled substance analog, as defined in K.S.A. 65-4159, prior to its repeal, K.S.A. 2010 Supp. 21-36a03, prior to its transfer, or K.S.A. 2022 Supp. 21-5703, and amendments thereto;

(B) Possession of ephedrine, pseudoephedrine, red phosphorus, lithium metal, sodium metal, iodine, anhydrous ammonia, pressurized ammonia or phenylpropanolamine, or their salts, isomers or salts of isomers with intent to use the product to manufacture a controlled substance, as defined in K.S.A. 65-7006(a), prior to its repeal, K.S.A. 2010 Supp. 21-36a09(a), prior to its transfer, or K.S.A. 2022 Supp. 21-5709(a), and amendments thereto;

(C)

(1) K.S.A. 65-4161, prior to its repeal, K.S.A. 2010 Supp. 21-36a05(a)(1), prior to its transfer, or K.S.A. 2022 Supp. 21-5705(a)(1), and amendments thereto. The provisions of this paragraph shall not apply

to violations of K.S.A. 2010 Supp. 21-36a05(a)(2) through (a)(6) or (b) that occurred on or after July 1, 2009, through April 15, 2010;

(2) Has been convicted of an offense that is comparable to any crime defined in this subsection, any out-of-state conviction for an offense that under the laws of this state would be an offense defined in this subsection; or

(3) Is or has been convicted of an attempt, conspiracy or criminal solicitation, as defined in K.S.A. 21-3301, 21-3302 or 21-3303, prior to their repeal, or K.S.A. 2022 Supp. 21-5301, 21-5302 and 21-5303, and amendments thereto, of an offense defined in this subsection.

(g) Convictions or adjudications that result from or are connected with the same act, or result from crimes committed at the same time, shall be counted for the purpose of this section as one conviction or adjudication. Any conviction or adjudication set aside pursuant to law is not a conviction or adjudication for purposes of this section. A conviction or adjudication from any out-of-state court shall constitute a conviction or adjudication for purposes of this section.

(h) "School" means any public or private educational institution, including, but not limited to, postsecondary school, college, university, community college, secondary school, high school, junior high school, middle school, elementary school, trade school, vocational school or professional school providing training or education to an offender for three or more consecutive days or parts of days, or for 10 or more nonconsecutive days in a period of 30 consecutive days.

(i) "Employment" means any full-time, part-time, transient, day-labor employment or volunteer work, with or without compensation, for three or more consecutive days or parts of days, or for 10 or more nonconsecutive days in a period of 30 consecutive days.

(j) "Reside" means to stay, sleep or maintain with regularity or temporarily one's person and property in a particular place other than a location where the offender is incarcerated. It shall be presumed that an offender resides at any and all locations where the offender stays, sleeps or maintains the offender's person for three or more consecutive days or parts of days, or for ten or more nonconsecutive days in a period of 30 consecutive days.

(k) "Residence" means a particular and definable place where an individual resides. Nothing in the Kansas offender registration act shall be construed to state that an offender may only have one residence for the purpose of such act.

(l) "Transient" means having no fixed or identifiable residence.

(m) "Law enforcement agency having initial jurisdiction" means the registering law enforcement agency of the county or location of jurisdiction where the offender expects to most often reside upon the offender's discharge, parole or release.

(n) "Registering law enforcement agency" means the sheriff's office or tribal police department responsible for registering an offender.

(o) "Registering entity" means any person, agency or other governmental unit, correctional facility or registering law enforcement agency responsible for obtaining the required information from, and explaining the required registration procedures to, any person required to register pursuant to the Kansas offender registration act. "Registering entity" includes, but is not limited to, sheriff's offices, tribal police departments and correctional facilities.

(p) "Treatment facility" means any public or private facility or institution providing inpatient mental health, drug or alcohol treatment or counseling, but does not include a hospital, as defined in K.S.A. 65-425, and amendments thereto.

(q) "Correctional facility" means any public or private correctional facility, juvenile detention facility, prison or jail.

(r) "Out-of-state" means: the District of Columbia; any federal, military or tribal jurisdiction, including those within this state; any foreign jurisdiction; or any state or territory within the United States, other than this state.

(s) "Duration of registration" means the length of time during which an offender is required to register for a specified offense or violation.

(t)
    (1) Notwithstanding any other provision of this section, "offender" shall not include any person who is:
        (A) Convicted of unlawful transmission of a visual depiction of a child, as defined in K.S.A. 2022 Supp. 21-5611(a), and amendments thereto, aggravated unlawful transmission of a visual depiction of a child, as defined in K.S.A. 2022 Supp. 21-5611(b), and amendments thereto, or unlawful possession of a visual depiction of a

child, as defined in K.S.A. 2022 Supp. 21-5610, and amendments thereto;

(B) Adjudicated as a juvenile offender for an act which, if committed by an adult, would constitute the commission of a crime defined in subsection (t)(1)(A);

(C) Adjudicated as a juvenile offender for an act which, if committed by an adult, would constitute the commission of sexual extortion as defined in K.S.A. 2022 Supp. 21-5515, and amendments thereto; or

(D) Adjudicated as a juvenile offender for an act which, if committed by an adult, would constitute a violation of K.S.A. 2022 Supp. 21-6101(a)(6), (a)(7) or (a)(8), and amendments thereto.

(2) Notwithstanding any other provision of law, a court shall not order any person to register under the Kansas offender registration act for the offenses described in subsection (t)(1).

22-4903. Violation of act; aggravated violation; penalties; new and separate offense; prosecution, venue.

(a) Violation of the Kansas offender registration act is the failure by an offender, as defined in K.S.A. 22-4902, and amendments thereto, to comply with any and all provisions of such act, including any and all duties set forth in K.S.A. 22-4905 through 22-4907, and amendments thereto. Any violation of the Kansas offender registration act which continues for more than 30 consecutive days shall, upon the 31st consecutive day, constitute a new and separate offense, and shall continue to constitute a new and separate offense every 30 days thereafter for as long as the violation continues.

(b) Aggravated violation of the Kansas offender registration act is violation of the Kansas offender registration act which continues for more than 180 consecutive days. Any aggravated violation of the Kansas offender registration act which continues for more than 180 consecutive days shall, upon the 181st consecutive day, constitute a new and separate offense, and shall continue to constitute a new and separate violation of the Kansas offender registration act every 30 days thereafter, or a new and separate aggravated violation of the Kansas offender registration act every 180 days thereafter, for as long as the violation continues.

(c)

(1) Except as provided in subsection (c)(3), violation of the Kansas offender registration act is:

(A) Upon a first conviction, a severity level 6 felony;

(B) Upon a second conviction, a severity level 5 felony; and

(C) Upon a third or subsequent conviction, a severity level 3 felony. Such violation shall be designated as a person or nonperson crime in accordance with the designation assigned to the underlying crime for which the offender is required to be registered under the Kansas offender registration act. If the offender is required to be registered under both a person and nonperson underlying crime, the violation shall be designated as a person crime.

(2) Except as provided in subsection (c)(3), aggravated violation of the Kansas offender registration act is a severity level 3 felony. Such violation shall be designated as a person or nonperson crime in accordance with the designation assigned to the underlying crime for which the offender is required to be registered under the Kansas offender registration act. If the offender is required to be registered under both a person and nonperson underlying crime, the violation shall be designated as a person crime.

(3) Violation of the Kansas offender registration act or aggravated violation of the Kansas

offender registration act consisting only of failing to remit payment to the sheriff's office as required in K.S.A. 22-4905 (l), and amendments thereto, is:

(A) Except as provided in subsection (c)(3)(B), a class A misdemeanor if, within 15 days of registration, full payment is not remitted to the sheriff's office;

(B) A severity level 9 felony if, within 15 days of the most recent registration, two or more full payments have not been remitted to the sheriff's office.

Such violation shall be designated as a person or nonperson crime in accordance with the designation assigned to the underlying crime for which the offender is required to be registered under the Kansas offender registration act. If the offender is required to be registered under both a person and nonperson underlying crime, the violation shall be designated as a person crime.

(d) Prosecution of violations of this section may be held:

(1) In any county in which the offender resides;

(2) In any county in which the offender is required to be registered under the Kansas offender registration act;

(3) In any county in which the offender is located during which time the offender is not in compliance with the Kansas offender registration act; or

(4) In the county in which any conviction or adjudication occurred for which the offender is required to be registered under the Kansas offender registration act.

K.S.A. 22-4904 **Registration of offender; duties of court, correctional facility, treatment facility, registering law enforcement agency, Kansas bureau of investigation, attorney general;**

Pre-Release: Reintegration

notification of schools and licensed child care facilities.

(a)

   (1) At the time of conviction or adjudication for an offense requiring registration as provided in K.S.A. 22-4902, and amendments thereto, the court shall:

      (A) Inform any offender, on the record, of the procedure to register and the requirements of K.S.A. 22-4905, and amendments thereto; and

      (B) If the offender is released:

         (i) Complete a notice of duty to register, which shall include title and statute number of conviction or adjudication, date of conviction or adjudication, case number, county of conviction or adjudication, and the following offender information: Name, address, date of birth, social security number, race, ethnicity and gender;

(ii) Require the offender to read and sign the notice of duty to register, which shall include a statement that the requirements provided in this subsection have been explained to the offender;

(iii) Order the offender to report within three business days to the registering law enforcement agency in the county or tribal land of conviction or adjudication and to the registering law enforcement agency in any place where the offender resides, maintains employment or attends school, to complete the registration form with all information and any updated information required for registration as provided in K.S.A. 22-4907, and amendments thereto; and

  (iv) Provide one copy of the notice of duty to register to the offender and, within three business days, send a copy of the form to the law enforcement agency having initial jurisdiction and to the Kansas bureau of investigation.

(2) At the time of sentencing or disposition for an offense requiring registration as provided in K.S.A. 22-4902, and amendments thereto, the court shall ensure the age of the victim is documented in the journal entry of conviction or adjudication.

(3) Upon commitment for control, care and treatment by the Kansas department for aging and disability services pursuant to K.S.A. 59-29a07, and amendments thereto, the court shall notify the registering law enforcement agency of the county where the offender resides during commitment of such offender's commitment. Such notice shall be prepared by the office of the attorney general for transmittal by the court by electronic means, including by fax or e-mail.

(b) The staff of any correctional facility or the registering law enforcement agency's designee shall:

(1) At the time of initial custody, register any offender within three business days:

(A) Inform the offender of the procedure for registration and of the offender's registration requirements as provided in K.S.A. 22-4905, and amendments thereto;

(B) Complete the registration form with all information and updated information required for registration as provided in K.S.A. 22-4907, and amendments thereto;

(C) Require the offender to read and sign the registration form, which shall include a statement that the requirements provided in this subsection have been explained to the offender;

(D) Provide one copy of the form to the offender and, within three business days, send a copy of the form to the Kansas bureau of investigation; and

(E) Enter all offender information required by the national crime information center into the national sex offender registry system within three business days of completing the registration or electronically submit all information and updated information required for registration as provided in K.S.A. 22-4907, and amendments thereto, within three business days to the Kansas bureau of investigation;

(2) Notify the Kansas Bureau of Investigation of the incarceration of any offender and of the location or any change in location of the offender while in custody;

(3) Prior to any offender being discharged, paroled, furloughed or released on work or school release that does not require the daily return to a correctional facility:

    (A) Inform the offender of the procedure for registration and of the offender's registration requirements as provided in K.S.A. 22-4905, and amendments thereto;

    (B) Complete the registration form with all information and updated information required for registration as provided in

K.S.A. 22-4907, and amendments thereto;

(C) Require the offender to read and sign the registration form, which shall include a statement that the requirements provided in this subsection have been explained to the offender;

(D) Photograph the offender's face and any identifying marks;

(E) Obtain fingerprint and palm prints of the offender; and

(F) Provide one copy of the form to the offender and, within three business days, send a copy of the form and of the photograph or photographs to the law enforcement agency having initial jurisdiction and to the Kansas bureau of investigation; and

(4) Notify the law enforcement agency having initial jurisdiction and the Kansas bureau of

investigation seven business days prior to any offender being discharged, paroled, furloughed or released on work or school release.

(c) The staff of any treatment facility shall:

(1) Within three business days of an offender's arrival for inpatient treatment, inform the registering law enforcement agency of the county or location of jurisdiction in which the treatment facility is located of the offender's presence at the treatment facility and the expected duration of the treatment, and immediately notify the registering law enforcement agency of an unauthorized or unexpected absence of the offender during the offender's treatment;

(2) Inform the registering law enforcement agency of the county or location of jurisdiction in which the treatment facility is located within three business days of an offender's discharge or release; and

Pre-Release: Reintegration

    (3)   Provide information upon request to any registering law enforcement agency having jurisdiction relevant to determining the presence of an offender within the treatment facility.

(d)   The registering law enforcement agency, upon the reporting of any offender, shall:

    (1)   Inform the offender of the duty to register as provided by the Kansas offender registration act;

    (2)

        (A)   Explain the procedure for registration and the offender's registration requirements as provided in K.S.A. 22-4905, and amendments thereto;

        (B)   Obtain the information required for registration as provided in K.S.A. 22-4907, and amendments thereto; and

        (C)   Require the offender to read and sign the registration form, which shall include a statement that the requirements provided in this subsection have been explained to the offender;

(3) Complete the registration form with all information and updated information required for registration, as provided in K.S.A. 22-4907, and amendments thereto, each time the offender reports to the registering law enforcement agency. All information and updated information reported by an offender shall be forwarded to the Kansas bureau of investigation within three business days;

(4) Maintain the original signed registration form, provide one copy of the completed registration form to the offender and, within three business days, send one copy of the completed form to the Kansas bureau of investigation;

(5) Forward a copy of any certified letter used for reporting pursuant to K.S.A. 22-4905, and amendments thereto, when utilized, within

Pre-Release: Reintegration

three business days to the Kansas bureau of investigation;

(6) Obtain registration information from every offender required to register regardless of whether or not the offender remits payment;

(7) Upon every required reporting, update the photograph or photographs of the offender's face and any new identifying marks and immediately forward copies or electronic files of the photographs to the Kansas bureau of investigation;

(8) Enter all offender information required by the national crime information center into the national sex offender registry system within three business days of completing the registration or electronically submit all information and updated information required for registration as provided in K.S.A. 22-4907, and amendments thereto, within three business days to the Kansas bureau of investigation;

(9) Maintain a special fund for the deposit and maintenance of fees paid by offenders. All funds retained by the registering law enforcement agency pursuant to the provisions of this section shall be credited to a special fund of the registering law enforcement agency which shall be used solely for law enforcement and criminal prosecution purposes and which shall not be used as a source of revenue to reduce the amount of funding otherwise made available to the registering law enforcement agency; and

(10) Forward any initial registration and updated registration information within three business days to any out of state jurisdiction where the offender is expected to reside, maintain employment or attend school.

(e)

(1) The Kansas bureau of investigation shall:

(A) Forward all additions or changes in information to any registering law

Pre-Release: Reintegration

enforcement agency, other than the agency that submitted the form, where the offender expects to reside, maintain employment or attend school;

(B) Ensure that offender information is immediately entered in the state registered offender database and the Kansas registered offender website, as provided in K.S.A. 22-4909, and amendments thereto;

(C) Transmit offender conviction or adjudication data, fingerprints and palm prints to the federal bureau of investigation; and

(D) Ensure all offender information required by the national crime information center is transmitted into the national sex offender registry system within three business days of such information being electronically submitted to the Kansas bureau of investigation.

(2) The director of the Kansas bureau of investigation may adopt rules and regulations necessary to implement the provisions of the Kansas offender registration act.

(f) The attorney general shall, within 10 business days of an offender being declared a sexually violent predator, forward to the Kansas bureau of investigation all relevant court documentation declaring an offender a sexually violent predator.

(g) The state department of education shall annually notify any school of the Kansas bureau of investigation internet website, and any internet website containing information on the Kansas offender registration act sponsored or created by the registering law enforcement agency of the county or location of jurisdiction in which the school is located, for the purpose of locating offenders who reside near such school. Such notification shall include information that the registering law enforcement agency of the county or location of jurisdiction where such school is located is available to the school to assist in using the registry and providing additional information on registered offenders.

(h) The secretary of health and environment shall annually notify any licensed child care facility of the Kansas bureau of investigation internet website, and any internet website containing information on the Kansas offender registration sponsored or created by the registering law enforcement agency of the county in which the facility is located, for the purpose of locating offenders who reside near such facility. Such notification shall include information that the registering law enforcement agency of the county or location of jurisdiction where such child care facility is located is available to the child care facilities to assist in using the registry and providing additional information on registered offenders.

(i) Upon request, the clerk of any court of record shall provide the Kansas bureau of investigation copies of complaints, indictments, information, journal entries, commitment orders or any other documents necessary to the performance of the duties of the Kansas bureau of investigation under the Kansas offender registration act. No fees or charges for providing such documents may be assessed.

K.S.A. 22-4905 **Duties of offender required to register; reporting; updated photograph; fee; driver's license; identification card.**

Any offender required to register as provided in the Kansas offender registration act shall:

(a) Except as otherwise provided in this subsection, register in person with the registering law enforcement agency within three business days of coming into any county or location of jurisdiction in which the offender resides or intends to reside, maintains employment or intends to maintain employment, or attends school or intends to attend school. Any such offender who cannot physically register in person with the registering law enforcement agency for such reasons including, but not limited to, incapacitation or hospitalization, as determined by a person licensed to practice medicine or surgery, or involuntarily committed pursuant to the Kansas sexually violent predator act, shall be subject to verification requirements other than in-person registration, as determined by the registering law enforcement agency having jurisdiction;

(b) Except as provided further, for any: (1) Sex offender, including a violent offender or drug offender who is also a sex offender, report in person four times each year to the registering law enforcement agency in the county or location of jurisdiction in which the offender resides, maintains employment or is attending a school; and (2) violent offender or drug offender, report in person four times each year to the registering law enforcement agency in the county or location of jurisdiction in which the offender resides, maintains employment or is attending a school, except that, at the discretion of the registering law enforcement agency, one of the four required reports may be conducted by certified letter. When utilized, the certified letter for reporting shall be sent by the registering law enforcement agency to the reported residence of the offender. The offender shall indicate any changes in information as required for reporting in person. The offender shall respond by returning the certified letter to the registering law enforcement agency within 10 business days by certified mail. The offender shall be required to report to the registering law enforcement agency once during the month of the offender's birthday and every third, sixth and ninth month occurring before and after the month of the offender's birthday. The registering law enforcement agency may determine the appropriate times and days for reporting by the offender, consistent with this subsection. Nothing contained in this subsection shall be construed to alleviate any offender from meeting the requirements prescribed in the Kansas offender registration act;

(c) Provide the information required for registration as provided in K.S.A. 22-4907, and amendments thereto, and verify all information previously provided is accurate;

(d) If in the custody of a correctional facility, register with the correctional facility within three business days of initial custody and shall not be required to update such registration until discharged, paroled, furloughed or released on work or school release from a correctional facility. A copy of the registration form and any updated registrations for an offender released on work or school release shall be sent, within three business days, to the registering law enforcement agency where the offender is incarcerated, maintains employment or attends school, and to the Kansas bureau of investigation;

(e) If involuntarily committed pursuant to the Kansas sexually violent predator act, register within three business days of arrival in the county where the offender resides during commitment. The offender shall not be required to update such registration until placed in a reintegration facility, on transitional release or on conditional release. Upon placement in a reintegration facility, on transitional release or on conditional release, the offender shall be personally responsible for complying with the provisions of the Kansas offender registration act;

(f) Notwithstanding subsections (a) and (b), if the offender is transient, report in person to the registering law enforcement agency of such county or location of jurisdiction in which the offender is physically present within three business days of arrival in the county or location of jurisdiction. Such offender shall be required to register in person with the registering law enforcement agency every 30 days, or more often at the discretion of the registering law enforcement agency. Such offender shall comply with the provisions of the Kansas offender registration act and, in addition, shall:

(1) Provide a list of places where the offender has slept and otherwise frequented during the period of time since the last date of registration; and

(2) Provide a list of places where the offender may be contacted and where the offender intends to sleep and otherwise frequent during the period of time prior to the next required date of registration;

(g) If required by out of state law, register in any out of state jurisdiction, where the offender resides, maintains employment or attends school;

(h) Register in person upon any commencement, change or termination of residence location, employment status, school attendance or other information as provided in K.S.A. 22-4907, and amendments thereto, within three business days of such commencement, change or termination, to the registering law enforcement agency or agencies where last registered and provide written notice to the Kansas bureau of investigation;

(i) Report in person to the registering law enforcement agency or agencies within three business days of any change in name;

(j) If receiving inpatient treatment at any treatment facility, inform the treatment facility of the offender's status as an offender and inform the registering law enforcement agency of the county or location of jurisdiction in which the treatment facility is located of the offender's presence at the treatment facility and the expected duration of the treatment;

(k) Submit to the taking of an updated photograph by the registering law enforcement agency on each occasion when the offender registers with or reports to the registering law enforcement agency in the county or location of jurisdiction in which the offender resides, maintains employment or attends school. In addition, such offender shall submit to the taking of a photograph to document any changes in identifying characteristics, including, but not limited to, scars, marks and tattoos;

(l) Remit payment to the sheriff's office in the amount of $20 as part of the reporting process required pursuant to subsection (b) in each county in which the offender resides, maintains employment or is attending school. Registration will be completed regardless of whether or not the offender remits payment. Failure of the offender to remit full payment within 15 days of registration is a violation of the Kansas offender registration act and is subject to prosecution pursuant to K.S.A. 22-4903, and amendments thereto. Notwithstanding other provisions herein, payment of this fee is not required:

   (1) When an offender provides updates or changes in information or during an initial registration unless such updates, changes or initial registration is during the month of such offender's birthday and every third,

sixth and ninth month occurring before and after the month of the offender's birthday;

(2) When an offender is transient and is required to register every 30 days, or more frequently as ordered by the registering law enforcement agency, except during the month of the offender's birthday and every third, sixth and ninth month occurring before and after the month of the offender's birthday; or

(3) If an offender has, prior to the required reporting and within the last three years, been determined to be indigent by a court of law, and the basis for that finding is recorded by the court;

(m) Annually renew any driver's license pursuant to K.S.A. 8-247, and amendments thereto, and annually renew any identification card pursuant to K.S.A. 2015 Supp. 8-1325a, and amendments thereto;

(n) If maintaining primary residence in this state, surrender all driver's licenses and identification cards from other states, territories and the District of Columbia, except if the offender is presently serving and maintaining active duty in any branch of the United States military or the offender is an immediate family member of a person presently serving and maintaining active duty in any branch of the United States military;

(o) Read and sign the registration form noting whether the requirements provided in this section have been explained to the offender; and

(p) Report in person to the registering law enforcement agency in the jurisdiction of the offender's residence and provide written notice to the Kansas bureau of investigation 21 days prior to any travel outside of the United States, and provide an itinerary including, but not limited to, destination, means of transport and duration of travel, or if under emergency circumstances, within three business days of making travel arrangements.

K.S.A. 22-4906 **Time period in which required to register; termination of registration requirement.**

(a)

    (1) Except as provided in subsection (c), if convicted of any of the following offenses, an offender's duration of registration shall be, if confined, 15 years after the date of parole, discharge or release, whichever date is most recent, or, if not confined, 15 years from the date of conviction:

        (A) Sexual battery, as defined in K.S.A. 21-3517, prior to its repeal, or K.S.A. 2022 Supp. 21-5505(a), and amendments thereto;

        (B) Adultery, as defined in K.S.A. 21-3507, prior to its repeal, or K.S.A. 2022 Supp. 21-5511, and amendments thereto,

(C) when one of the parties involved is less than 18 years of age;

(C) Promoting the sale of sexual relations, as defined in K.S.A. 2022 Supp. 21-6420, and amendments thereto;

(D) Patronizing a prostitute, as defined in K.S.A. 21-3515, prior to its repeal, or K.S.A. 2022 Supp. 21-6421, prior to its amendment by section 18 of chapter 120 of the 2013 Session Laws of Kansas on July 1, 2013, when one of the parties involved is less than 18 years of age;

(E) Lewd and lascivious behavior, as defined in K.S.A. 21-3508, prior to its repeal, or K.S.A. 2022 Supp. 21-5513, and amendments thereto, when one of the parties involved is less than 18 years of age;

(F) Capital murder, as defined in K.S.A. 21-3439, prior to its repeal, or K.S.A.

2022 Supp. 21-5401, and amendments thereto;

(G) Murder in the first degree, as defined in K.S.A. 21-3401, prior to its repeal, or K.S.A. 2022 Supp. 21-5402, and amendments thereto;

(H) Murder in the second degree, as defined in K.S.A. 21-3402, prior to its repeal, or K.S.A. 2022 Supp. 21-5403, and amendments thereto;

(I) Voluntary manslaughter, as defined in K.S.A. 21-3403, prior to its repeal, or K.S.A. 2022 Supp. 21-5404, and amendments thereto;

(J) Involuntary manslaughter, as defined in K.S.A. 21-3404, prior to its repeal, or K.S.A. 2022 Supp. 21-5405(a)(1), (a)(2) or (a)(4), and amendments thereto;

(K) Criminal restraint, as defined in K.S.A. 21-3424, prior to its repeal, or K.S.A. 2022 Supp. 21-5411, and amendments thereto, except by a parent, and only when the victim is less than 18 years of age;

(L) Sexual extortion, as defined in K.S.A. 2022 Supp. 21-5515, and amendments thereto, when one of the parties involved is less than 18 years of age;

(M) Breach of privacy, as defined in K.S.A. 2021 Supp. 21-6101(a) (6), (a)(7) or (a)(8), and amendments thereto;

(N) Any act that has been determined beyond a reasonable doubt to have been sexually motivated, unless the court, on the record, finds that the act involved non-forcible sexual conduct, the victim was at least 14 years of age and the offender was not more than four years older than the victim;

(O) Conviction of any person required by court order to register for an offense not otherwise required as provided in the Kansas offender registration act;

(P) Conviction of any person felony and the court makes a finding on the record that a deadly weapon was used in the commission of such person felony;

(Q) Unlawful manufacture or attempting such of any controlled substance or controlled substance analog, as defined in K.S.A. 65-4159, prior to its repeal, K.S.A. 2010 Supp. 21-36a03, prior to its transfer, or K.S.A. 2022 Supp. 21-5703, and amendments thereto;

(R) Possession of ephedrine, pseudoephedrine, red phosphorus, lithium metal, sodium metal, iodine, anhydrous ammonia, pressurized ammonia or phenylpropanolamine, or their salts, isomers or salts of isomers with intent to use the product to manufacture a controlled substance, as defined by K.S.A. 65-7006(a), prior to its repeal, K.S.A. 2010 Supp. 21-36a09(a), prior to its transfer, or K.S.A. 2022 Supp. 21-5709(a), and amendments thereto;

(S) K.S.A. 65-4161, prior to its repeal, K.S.A. 2010 Supp. 21-36a05(a)(1), prior to its transfer, or K.S.A. 2022 Supp. 21-5705(a)(1), and amendments thereto; or

(T) Any attempt, conspiracy or criminal solicitation, as defined in K.S.A. 21-3301, 21-3302 or 21-3303, prior to their repeal, or K.S.A. 2022 Supp. 21-5301, 21-5302 and 21-5303, and amendments thereto, of an offense defined in this subsection.

(2) Except as otherwise provided by the Kansas offender registration act, the duration of registration terminates, if not confined, at the

Pre-Release: Reintegration

expiration of 15 years from the date of conviction. Any period of time during which any offender is incarcerated in any jail or correctional facility or during which the offender does not comply with any and all requirements of the Kansas offender registration act shall not count toward the duration of registration.

(b)

(1) Except as provided in subsection (c), if convicted of any of the following offenses, an offender's duration of registration shall be, if confined, 25 years after the date of parole, discharge or release, whichever date is most recent, or, if not confined, 25 years from the date of conviction:

(A) Criminal sodomy, as defined in K.S.A. 21-3505(a)(1), prior to its repeal, or K.S.A. 2022 Supp. 21-5504(a)(1) or (a)(2), and amendments thereto, when one of the parties involved is less than 18 years of age;

(B) Indecent solicitation of a child, as defined in K.S.A. 21-3510, prior to its repeal, or K.S.A. 2022 Supp. 21-5508(a), and amendments thereto;

(C) Electronic solicitation, as defined in K.S.A. 21-3523, prior to its repeal, or K.S.A. 2022 Supp. 21-5509, and amendments thereto;

(D) Aggravated incest, as defined in K.S.A. 21-3603, prior to its repeal, or K.S.A. 2022 Supp. 21-5604(b), and amendments thereto;

(E) Indecent liberties with a child, as defined in K.S.A. 21-3503, prior to its repeal, or K.S.A. 2022 Supp. 21-5506(a), and amendments thereto;

(F) Unlawful sexual relations, as defined in K.S.A. 21-3520, prior to its repeal, or

	K.S.A. 2021 Supp. 21-5512, and amendments thereto;
(G)	Sexual exploitation of a child, as defined in K.S.A. 21-3516, prior to its repeal, or K.S.A. 2022 Supp. 21-5510, and amendments thereto, if the victim is 14 or more years of age but less than 18 years of age;
(H)	Aggravated sexual battery, as defined in K.S.A. 21-3518, prior to its repeal, or K.S.A. 2022 Supp. 21-5505(b), and amendments thereto;
(I)	Internet trading in child pornography, as defined in K.S.A. 2022 Supp. 21-5514, and amendments thereto;
(J)	Aggravated internet trading in child pornography, as defined in K.S.A. 2022 Supp. 21-5514, and amendments thereto, if the victim is 14 or more years of age but less than 18 years of age;

(K) Promoting prostitution, as defined in K.S.A. 21-3513, prior to its repeal, or K.S.A. 2022 Supp. 21-6420, prior to its amendment by section 17 of chapter 120 of the 2013 Session Laws of Kansas on July 1, 2013, if the person selling sexual relations is 14 or more years of age but less than 18 years of age; or

(L) Any attempt, conspiracy or criminal solicitation, as defined in K.S.A. 21-3301, 21-3302 or 21-3303, prior to their repeal, or K.S.A. 2022 Supp. 21-5301, 21-5302 and 21-5303, and amendments thereto, of an offense defined in this subsection.

(2) Except as otherwise provided by the Kansas offender registration act, the duration of registration terminates, if not confined, at the expiration of 25 years from the date of conviction. Any period of time during which

any offender is incarcerated in any jail or correctional facility or during which the offender does not comply with any and all requirements of the Kansas offender registration act shall not count toward the duration of registration.

(c) Upon a second or subsequent conviction of an offense requiring registration, an offender's duration of registration shall be for such offender's lifetime.

(d) The duration of registration for any offender who has been convicted of any of the following offenses shall be for such offender's lifetime:

(1) Rape, as defined in K.S.A. 21-3502, prior to its repeal, or K.S.A. 2022 Supp. 21-5503, and amendments thereto;

(2) Aggravated indecent solicitation of a child, as defined in K.S.A. 21-3511, prior to its repeal, or K.S.A. 2022 Supp. 21-5508(b), and amendments thereto;

(3) Aggravated indecent liberties with a child, as defined in K.S.A. 21-3504, prior to its repeal, or K.S.A. 2022 Supp. 21-5506(b), and amendments thereto;

(4) Criminal sodomy, as defined in K.S.A. 21-3505(a)(2) or (a)(3), prior to its repeal, or K.S.A. 2022 Supp. 21-5504(a)(3) or (a)(4), and amendments thereto;

(5) Aggravated criminal sodomy, as defined in K.S.A. 21-3506, prior to its repeal, or K.S.A. 2022 Supp. 21-5504(b), and amendments thereto;

(6) Aggravated human trafficking, as defined in K.S.A. 21-3447, prior to its repeal, or K.S.A. 2022 Supp. 21-5426(b), and amendments thereto;

(7) Sexual exploitation of a child, as defined in K.S.A. 21-3516, prior to its repeal, or K.S.A. 2022 Supp. 21-5510, and amendments thereto, if the victim is less than 14 years of age;

(8) Promoting prostitution, as defined in K.S.A. 21-3513, prior to its repeal, or K.S.A. 2022 Supp. 21-6420, prior to its amendment by section 17 of chapter 120 of the 2013 Session Laws of Kansas on July 1, 2013, if the person selling sexual relations is less than 14 years of age;

(9) Kidnapping, as defined in K.S.A. 21-3420, prior to its repeal, or K.S.A. 2022 Supp. 21-5408(a), and amendments thereto;

(10) Aggravated kidnapping, as defined in K.S.A. 21-3421, prior to its repeal, or K.S.A. 2022 Supp. 21-5408(b), and amendments thereto;

(11) Aggravated internet trading in child pornography, as defined in K.S.A. 2022 Supp. 21-5514, and amendments thereto, if the victim is less than 14 years of age;

(12) Commercial sexual exploitation of a child, as defined in K.S.A. 2022 Supp. 21-6422, and amendments thereto; or

(13) Any attempt, conspiracy or criminal solicitation, as defined in K.S.A. 21-3301, 21-3302 or 21-3303, prior to their repeal, or K.S.A. 2022 Supp. 21-5301, 21-5302 and 21-5303, and amendments thereto, of an offense defined in this subsection.

(e) Any person who has been declared a sexually violent predator pursuant to K.S.A. 59-29a01 et seq., and amendments thereto, shall register for such person's lifetime.

(f) Notwithstanding any other provisions of this section, for an offender less than 14 years of age who is adjudicated as a juvenile offender for an act which, if committed by an adult, would constitute a sexually violent crime set forth in K.S.A. 22-4902(c), and amendments thereto, the court shall:

(1) Require registration until such offender reaches 18 years of age, at the expiration of five years from the date of adjudication or, if confined, from release from confinement, whichever date occurs later. Any period of time during which the offender is incarcerated in any jail, juvenile facility or correctional facility or during which the offender does not comply with any and all requirements of the Kansas offender registration act shall not count toward the duration of registration;

(2) Not require registration if the court, on the record, finds substantial and compelling reasons therefore; or

(3) Require registration, but such registration information shall not be open to inspection by the public or posted on any internet website, as provided in K.S.A. 22-4909, and amendments thereto. If the court requires registration but such registration is not open to the public, such offender shall provide a copy of such court order to the registering law enforcement agency at the time of registration. The registering law enforcement agency shall forward a copy of such court order to the Kansas bureau of investigation.

If such offender violates a condition of release during the term of the conditional release, the court may require such offender to register pursuant to paragraph (1).

(g) Notwithstanding any other provisions of this section, for an offender 14 years of age or more who is adjudicated as a juvenile offender for an act which, if committed by an adult, would constitute a sexually violent crime set forth in K.S.A. 22-4902(c), and amendments thereto, and such crime is not an off-grid felony or a felony ranked in severity level 1 of the nondrug grid as provided in K.S.A. 21-4704, prior to its repeal, or K.S.A. 2022 Supp. 21-6804, and amendments thereto, the court shall:

(1) Require registration until such offender reaches 18 years of age, at the expiration of five years from the date of adjudication or, if confined, from release from confinement, whichever date occurs later. Any period of time during which the offender is incarcerated in any jail, juvenile facility or correctional facility or during which the offender does not comply with any and all requirements of the Kansas offender registration act shall not count toward the duration of registration;

(2) Not require registration if the court, on the record, finds substantial and compelling reasons therefore; or

(3) Require registration, but such registration information shall not be open to inspection by the public or posted on any internet website, as provided in K.S.A. 22-4909, and amendments thereto. If the court requires registration but such registration is not open to the public, such offender shall provide a copy of such court order to the registering law enforcement agency

at the time of registration. The registering law enforcement agency shall forward a copy of such court order to the Kansas bureau of investigation.

If such offender violates a condition of release during the term of the conditional release, the court may require such offender to register pursuant to paragraph (1).

(h) Notwithstanding any other provisions of this section, an offender 14 years of age or more who is adjudicated as a juvenile offender for an act which, if committed by an adult, would constitute a sexually violent crime set forth in K.S.A. 22-4902(c), and amendments thereto, and such crime is an off-grid felony or a felony ranked in severity level 1 of the nondrug grid as provided in K.S.A. 21-4704, prior to its repeal, or K.S.A. 2022 Supp. 21-6804, and amendments thereto, shall be required to register for such offender's lifetime.

(i) Notwithstanding any other provision of law, if a diversionary agreement or probation order, either adult or juvenile, or a juvenile offender sentencing order, requires registration under the Kansas offender registration act for an offense that would not otherwise require registration as provided in K.S.A. 22-4902(a)(5), and amendments thereto, then all provisions of the Kansas offender registration act shall apply, except that the duration of registration shall be controlled by such diversionary agreement, probation order or juvenile offender sentencing order.

(j) The duration of registration does not terminate if the convicted or adjudicated offender again becomes liable to register as provided by the Kansas offender registration act during the required period of registration.

(k) For any person moving to Kansas who has been convicted or adjudicated in an out-of-state court, or who was required to register under an out-of-state law, the duration of registration shall be the length of time required by the out-of-state jurisdiction or by the Kansas offender registration act, whichever length of time is longer. The provisions of this subsection shall apply to convictions or adjudications prior to June 1,

2006, and to persons who moved to Kansas prior to June 1, 2006, and to convictions or adjudications on or after June 1, 2006, and to persons who moved to Kansas on or after June 1, 2006.

(l) For any person residing, maintaining employment or attending school in this state who has been convicted or adjudicated by an out-of-state court of an offense that is comparable to any crime requiring registration pursuant to the Kansas offender registration act, but who was not required to register in the jurisdiction of conviction or adjudication, the duration of registration shall be the duration required for the comparable offense pursuant to the Kansas offender registration act.

K.S.A. 22-4907   Information required in registration.

(a) Registration as required by the Kansas offender registration act shall consist of a form approved by the Kansas bureau of investigation, which shall include a statement that the requirements provided in this section have been reviewed and explained to the

Pre-Release: Reintegration

offender, and shall be signed by the offender and, except when such reporting is conducted by certified letter as provided in subsection (b) of K.S.A. 22-4905, and amendments thereto, witnessed by the person registering the offender. Such registration form shall include the following offender information:

(1) Name and all alias names;

(2) Date and city, state and country of birth, and any alias dates or places of birth;

(3) Title and statute number of each offense or offenses committed, date of each conviction or adjudication and court case numbers for each conviction or adjudication;

(4) City, county, state or country of conviction or adjudication;

(5) Sex and date of birth or purported age of each victim of all offenses requiring registration;

(6) Current residential address, any anticipated future residence and any temporary lodging information including, but not limited to, address, telephone number and dates of travel

for any place in which the offender is staying for seven or more days; and, if transient, the locations where the offender has stayed and frequented since last reporting for registration;

(7) All telephone numbers at which the offender may be contacted including, but not limited to, all mobile telephone numbers;

(8) Social security number, and all alias social security numbers;

(9) Identifying characteristics such as race, ethnicity, skin tone, sex, age, height, weight, hair and eye color, scars, tattoos and blood type;

(10) Occupation and name, address or addresses and telephone number of employer or employers, and name of any anticipated employer and place of employment;

(11) All current driver's licenses or identification cards, including a photocopy of all such driver's licenses or identification cards and

their numbers, states of issuance and expiration dates;

(12) All vehicle information, including the license plate number, registration number and any other identifier and description of any vehicle owned or operated by the offender, or any vehicle the offender regularly drives, either for personal use or in the course of employment, and information concerning the location or locations such vehicle or vehicles are habitually parked or otherwise kept;

(13) License plate number, registration number or other identifier and description of any aircraft or watercraft owned or operated by the offender, and information concerning the location or locations such aircraft or watercraft are habitually parked, docked or otherwise kept;

(14) All professional licenses, designations and certifications;

(15) Documentation of any treatment received for a mental abnormality or personality disorder of the offender; for purposes of documenting the treatment received, registering law enforcement agencies, correctional facility officials, treatment facility officials and courts may rely on information that is readily available to them from existing records and the offender;

(16) A photograph or photographs;

(17) Fingerprints and palm prints;

(18) Any and all schools and satellite schools attended or expected to be attended and the locations of attendance and telephone number;

(19) Any and all: E-mail addresses; online identities used by the offender on the internet; information relating to membership in any and all personal web pages or online social networks; and internet screen names;

(20) All travel and immigration documents; and

(21) Name and telephone number of the offender's probation, parole or community corrections officer.

(b) The offender shall provide biological samples for DNA analysis to the registering law enforcement agency as required by K.S.A. 21-2511, and amendments thereto. The biological samples shall be in the form using a DNA databank kit authorized by the Kansas bureau of investigation. The registering law enforcement agency shall forward such biological samples to the Kansas bureau of investigation. Prior to taking such sample, the registering law enforcement agency shall search the Kansas criminal justice information system to determine if such person's DNA profile is currently on file. If such person's DNA profile is on file with the Kansas bureau of investigation, the registering law enforcement agency is not required to take biological samples.

K.S.A. 22-4908   **Person required to register shall not be relieved of further registration.**

(a) Except as provided in subsection (b), a drug offender who is required to register under the Kansas offender registration act may file a verified petition for relief from registration requirements if the offender has registered for a period of at least five years after the date of parole, discharge or release, whichever date is most recent, or, if not confined, five years from the date of conviction or adjudication.

(b) An offender who is required to register pursuant to K.S.A. 22-4906(k), and amendments thereto, because of an out-of-state conviction or adjudication may not petition for relief from registration requirements in this state if the offender would be required to register under the law of the state or jurisdiction where the conviction or adjudication occurred. If the offender would no longer be required to register under the law of the state or jurisdiction where the conviction or adjudication occurred, the offender may file a verified petition pursuant to subsection (a).

(c) Any period of time during which an offender is incarcerated in any jail or correctional facility or during which the offender does not substantially comply with the requirements of the Kansas offender registration act shall not count toward the duration of registration required in subsection (a).

(d)
  (1) A verified petition for relief from registration requirements shall be filed in the district court in the county where the offender was convicted or adjudicated of the offense requiring registration. If the offender was not convicted or adjudicated in this state of the offense requiring registration, such petition shall be filed in the district court of any county where the offender is currently required to register. The docket fee shall be as provided in K.S.A. 60-2001, and amendments thereto.

  (2) The petition shall include:

   (A) The offender's full name;

(B) The offender's full name at the time of conviction or adjudication for the offense or offenses requiring registration, if different than the offender's current name;

(C) The offender's sex, race and date of birth;

(D) The offense or offenses requiring registration;

(E) The date of conviction or adjudication for the offense or offenses requiring registration;

(F) The court in which the offender was convicted or adjudicated of the offense or offenses requiring registration;

(G) Whether the offender has been arrested, convicted, adjudicated or entered into a diversion agreement for any crime during the period the offender is required to register; and

(H) The names of all treatment providers and agencies that have treated the offender for mental health, substance abuse and offense-related behavior since the date of the offense or offenses requiring registration.

(3) The judicial council shall develop a petition form for use under this section.

(4) When a petition is filed, the court shall set a date for a hearing on such petition and cause notice of the hearing to be given to the county or district attorney in the county where the petition is filed. Any person who may have relevant information about the offender may testify at the hearing.

(5) The county or district attorney shall notify any victim of the offense requiring registration who is alive and whose address is known or, if the victim is deceased, the victim's family if the family's address is known. The victim or

victim's family shall not be compelled to testify or provide any discovery to the offender.

(6) The county or district attorney shall have access to all applicable records, including records that are otherwise confidential or privileged.

(e)

(1) The court may require a drug offender who is petitioning for relief under this section to undergo a risk assessment.

(2) Any risk assessment ordered under this subsection shall be performed by a professional agreed upon by the parties or a professional approved by the court. Such risk assessment shall be performed at the offender's expense.

(f) The court shall order relief from registration requirements if the offender shows by clear and convincing evidence that:

(1) The offender has not been convicted or adjudicated of a felony, other than a felony

violation or aggravated felony violation of K.S.A. 22-4903, and amendments thereto, within the five years immediately preceding the filing of the petition, and no proceedings involving any such felony are presently pending or being instituted against the offender;

(2) The offender's circumstances, behavior and treatment history demonstrate that the offender is sufficiently rehabilitated to warrant relief; and

(3) Registration of the offender is no longer necessary to promote public safety.

(g) If the court denies an offender's petition for relief, the offender shall not file another petition for relief until three years have elapsed, unless a shorter time period is ordered by the court.

(h) If the court grants relief from registration requirements, the court shall order that the offender be removed from the offender registry and that the offender is no longer required to comply with registration requirements. Within 14 days of any order, the court shall notify the Kansas bureau of investigation and any local law enforcement agency that registers the offender that the offender has been granted relief from registration requirements. The Kansas bureau of investigation shall remove such offender from any internet website maintained pursuant to K.S.A. 22-4909, and amendments thereto.

(i) An offender may combine a petition for relief under this section with a petition for expungement under K.S.A. 2022 Supp. 21-6614, and amendments thereto, if the offense requiring registration is otherwise eligible for expungement.

K.S.A. 22-4909 **Information subject to open records act; website posting; exceptions; nondisclosure of certain information.**

(a) Except as prohibited by subsections (c), (d), (e) and (f) of this section and subsections (f) and (g) of K.S.A. 22-4906, and amendments thereto, the statements or any other information required by the Kansas offender registration act shall be open to inspection by the public at the registering law enforcement agency, at the headquarters of the Kansas bureau of investigation and on any internet website sponsored or created by a registering law enforcement agency or the Kansas bureau of investigation that contains such statements or information, and specifically are subject to the provisions of the Kansas open records act, K.S.A. 45-215 et seq., and amendments thereto.

(b) Any information posted on an internet website sponsored or created by a registering law enforcement agency or the Kansas bureau of investigation shall identify, in a prominent manner, whether an offender is a sex offender, a violent offender or a drug offender. Such internet websites shall include the following information for each offender:

(1) Name of the offender, including any aliases;

Pre-Release: Reintegration

(2) Address of each residence at which the offender resides or will reside and, if the offender does not have any present or expected residence address, other information about where the offender has their home or habitually lives. If current information of this type is not available because the offender is in violation of the requirement to register or cannot be located, the website must so note;

(3) Temporary lodging information;

(4) Address of any place where the offender is a student or will be a student;

(5) License plate number and a description of any vehicle owned or operated by the offender, including any aircraft or watercraft;

(6) Physical description of the offender;

(7) The offense or offenses for which the offender is registered and any other offense for which the offender has been convicted or adjudicated;

(8) A current photograph of the offender; and

(9) All professional licenses, designations and certifications.

(c) Notwithstanding subsection (a), information posted on an internet website sponsored or created by a registering law enforcement agency or the Kansas bureau of investigation shall not contain the address of any place where the offender is an employee or any other information about where the offender works. Such internet website shall contain a statement that employment information is publicly available and may be obtained by contacting the appropriate registering law enforcement agency or by signing up for community notification through the official website of the Kansas bureau of investigation.

(d) Notwithstanding subsection (a), pursuant to a court finding petitioned by the prosecutor, any offender who is required to register pursuant to the Kansas offender registration act, but has been provided a new identity and relocated under the federal witness security program or who has worked as a confidential informant, or is otherwise a protected witness, shall be required to register pursuant to the Kansas offender registration act, but shall not be subject to public registration.

(e) Notwithstanding subsection (a), when a court orders expungement of a conviction or adjudication that requires an offender to register pursuant to the Kansas offender registration act, the registration requirement for such conviction or adjudication does not terminate. Such offender shall be required to continue registering pursuant to the Kansas offender registration act, but shall not be subject to public registration. If a court orders expungement of a conviction or adjudication that requires an offender to register pursuant to the Kansas offender registration act, and the offender has any other conviction or adjudication that requires registration, such offender shall be required to register pursuant to the Kansas offender registration act, and the registration for such other conviction or adjudication shall be open to inspection by the public and shall be subject to the provisions of subsection (a), unless such registration has been ordered restricted pursuant to subsection (f) or (g) of K.S.A. 22-4906, and amendments thereto.

(f) Notwithstanding subsection (a), the following information shall not be disclosed other than to law enforcement agencies:

(1) The name, address, telephone number or any other information which specifically and individually identifies the identity of any victim of a registerable offense;

(2) The social security number of the offender;

(3) The offender's criminal history arrests that did not result in convictions or adjudications;

(4) Travel and immigration document numbers of the offender; and

(5) Internet identifiers of the offender.

K.S.A. 22-4910   **Effective date.**

K.S.A. 22-4901 through 22-4910 shall be effective on and after July 1, 1993.

K.S.A. 22-4911   **Cause of action; not created.**

Nothing in the Kansas offender registration act shall create a cause of action against the state or an employee of the state acting within the scope of the employee's employment as a result of requiring an offender to register or an offender's failure to register. This includes, but is not limited to, the person or persons assigned to a registering law enforcement agency to register offenders, and the person or persons assigned to enter all offender information required by the national crime information center into the national sex offender registry system.

K.S.A. 22-4913　　Offender residency restrictions; prohibition from adopting or enforcing; exceptions; definitions.

(a)　Except as provided in subsection (b), on and after June 1, 2006, cities and counties shall be prohibited from adopting or enforcing any ordinance, resolution or regulation establishing residential restrictions for offenders as defined by K.S.A. 22-4902, and amendments thereto.

(b) The prohibition in subsection (a), shall not apply to any city or county residential licensing or zoning program for correctional placement residences that includes regulations for the housing of such offenders.

(c) As used in this section, "correctional placement residence" means a facility that provides residential services for individuals or offenders who reside or have been placed in such facility due to any one of the following situations:

(1) Prior to, or instead of, being sentenced to prison;

(2) As a conditional release prior to a hearing;

(3) As a part of a sentence of confinement of not more than one year;

(4) In a privately operated facility housing parolees;

(5) As a deferred sentence when placed in a facility operated by community corrections;

(6) As a requirement of court-ordered treatment services for alcohol or drug abuse; or

(7) As part of voluntary treatment services for alcohol or drug abuse.

Correctional placement residence shall not include a single or multi-family dwelling or commercial residential building that provides a residence to staff and persons other than those described in paragraphs (1) through (7).

Chapter 3: Legal Battles Over KORA

The KORA seems pretty straightforward, however, during my time under the KSVPA there has been a few lawsuits concerning the KORA.

When I came to the facility under the KSVPA I did not register nor did anyone else. When KDADS took over for SRS, due to legislative reorganization, they requested that all two-hundred and fifty SVP's be registered. The request was made to the Pawnee County Sheriff.

The Pawnee County Sheriff refused to do his duties under the KORA and register those confined under the KSVPA. This was made publicly known when the Court of Appeals issued its decision in *Clark v. Keck*, 381 P.3d 519; 2016 WL 5867248.

KDADS then requested an opinion concerning the issue from the Kansas Attorney General. The Attorney General held that the Pawnee County Sheriff was in violation of the KORA for he had a duty and obligation to ensure registration of those confined under the KSVPA. Attorney General Opinion 2016-1.

After all of this the Pawnee County Sheriff then went to the Kansas Legislature and requested a law change. The Sheriff sought that the amendment would relieve him of the burden of having to register those confined under the KSVPA. The Legislature granted the amendment and now one only has to register upon commitment.

The individual does not come under the KSVPA until they are released to Reintegration, Transition, Conditional or Final Discharge.

This then spawned a new suit when the author was returned from Reintegration. The author argued that per K.S.A. 22-4905(m) he was required to annually renew his State ID/Driver's license or be in violation of the KORA.

KDADS argued that the amendment that the Sheriff had put in place negates the requirement to annually renew any State ID or Driver's license and thereby denied Mr. Merryfield the ability to renew.

After exhausting internal remedies Mr. Merryfield then took it to the Pawnee County District Court, wherein Judge Bruce T. Gatterman held that there is no requirement to annually renew the ID/License per the amendment put in place after the Sheriff's request.

A few months after receiving the decision the facility allowed Mr. Merryfield to get a State ID. Upon receiving it the Kansas Department of Revenue, Division of Motor Vehicles (DMV), informed him that as a registered offender he was required to renew it once per year.

Mr. Merryfield then submitted a copy of Judge Gatterman's ruling and a letter to the DMV and the response received was that K.S.A. 22-4905(m) requires annual renewal. Mr. Merryfield then sent a second letter to the DMV and one to the Kansas Attorney General. The response received was that Judge Gatterman's order was improper and there is no exception to the provisions found in K.S.A. 22-4905(m).

It is still unclear as to whether or not annual renewal is required and if not done what would or could occur to Mr. Merryfield. What is known is that all State Actors (KDADS, Sheriff, Judge, Attorney General, and DMV) involved, each have their own interpretation and they are not the same. They also request and get the Legislature to bend or change the law to fit their needs.

Pre-Release: Reintegration

How does this serve the intent and purpose of the KORA. It cannot be said that it does for now there is a group of sex offenders that are not listed. However, these are the most dangerous of all sex offenders in Kansas, as the Legislature declared so in the preamble of the KSVPA. Thus, ignoring the law because of inconvenience is wrong.

Then we must look at the message it provides to criminals. If you are in power, have the ability to control the lawmakers, you can do whatever you want with any law. This cannot be what the taxpayer dollars are used to pay these employees of the citizens, or is it what we as a society want?

We should expect more of those paid with taxpayer dollars. They have done nothing more than prevent the KORA from being fully effective.

Pre-Release: Reintegration

Chapter 4: The Cost of KORA

The KORA requires many hours of labor to maintain and operate, where does the money come from? The simplest answer is that the taxpayers pay for it and then it is subsidized by the one required to register.

The person required to register has to pay twenty dollars each time he/she registers., a total of eighty dollars per year.

In addition to this one under the KORA is required to annually renew their driver's license or state ID. By paying yearly the registered offender pays more than double the cost a normal citizen would for the same driver's license or state ID.

As an example let's look to one who has been on the registry for ten years. This means he has paid the twenty dollars forty times for a total of eight-hundred dollars. Then he has renewed his state ID or driver's license ten times at a cost of twelve dollars each, for a grand total of one-hundred and twenty dollars. Basically every ten years the state makes one-thousand dollars off of the person.

If the State of Kansas has one-thousand on the registry they reap one million dollars every ten years. This is in addition to the funds provided by the taxpayers. I look at this as another way to reap rewards at the expense of others. However, we must remember that the KORA is not to be punitive, so it cannot be said that this is the cost of doing crime.

Final Thoughts

We have journeyed through many laws and questionable behaviors in this book by looking honestly at what KDADS calls Reintegration. Each person will decide on their own whether it is right or wrong.

For me I found some guidance from the decision of an open-minded judge in Kansas, the Honorable Jeffry L Jack, Labette County Court. The Judge's opinion included the following paragraphs.

"Under the procedural scheme set out in K.S.A. 59-29a08, at the annual hearing under subsection (d) if the court finds probable cause that the committed person's mental abnormality or personality disorder has significantly changed so that the person is safe to be placed in transitional release, then there is a hearing on transitional release under subsection (g). if the State fails to prove beyond a reasonable doubt that the person's mental abnormality disorder remains such that that the person is not safe to be placed in transitional release, then the court may place the person in transitional release."

"However, once in transitional release, the treatment staff (**_who are not disinterested parties_**) may determine a violation of a rule, regulation, or directive under subsection (j) and the state then has only to show probable cause that a person violated a rule of transitional release at a hearing under subsection (k) to return that person to a secure commitment facility. Of course, then there will be another annual hearing under (d), and the committed person has already, at the prior annual hearing, shown probable cause that the person's mental abnormality or personality disorder has improved, so the court moves him back to transitional release under (g)." [Emphasis (bold, underline, italics) was added]

"The result is a **_game of table tennis_**, where the person bounces back and forth between the secure commitment facility and transitional release because the State cannot meet the higher burden to keep him in the secure commitment facility under subsection (g), but can easily meet the lower burden to return him there under subsections (j) and (k), and the committed person can continue to meet the burden to return to transitional release under subsections (d) and (g)." [Emphasis (bold, underline, italics) was added]

The Judge was spot on with not only my personal experience but also with the facts that I see every day whereby one goes to Reintegration and a few months later is returned for a rule violation. Never have they been returned for a relapse. Then those individuals go to reintegration and are returned again.

For the individuals in the program they see and call Reintegration the revolving door. One goes and one comes back constantly. If the PRP was correct and the person had changed why are they being returned?

In order to go to Reintegration one must complete the program and be found by the PRP to have nothing left to complete. How then is this all undone by a rule violation? That is a good question.

Then what is the danger to society by KDADS ignoring the law and doing as they please with Reintegration? This is a valid question illustrated and shown throughout this book.

Ultimately if you feel that a change is needed you may contact the appropriate official and formally request the change.

For the time being I thank you for taking the time to read this book and any action you may take. I know it is not a popular subject, but keeping the public in the dark is just as dangerous. I am glad to be a beacon in the night highlighting and showing what the truth is.

I look forward to releasing future books on the KSVPA that allows the public to know more.

Pre-Release: Reintegration

www.ingramcontent.com/pod-product-compliance
Lightning Source LLC
Chambersburg PA
CBHW051523020426
42333CB00016B/1751